Occasional Paper No. 50

# Strengthening the International Monetary System: Exchange Rates, Surveillance, and Objective Indicators

By Andrew Crockett and Morris Goldstein

International Monetary Fund
Washington, D.C.
February 1987

© 1987 International Monetary Fund

**Library of Congress Cataloging-in-Publication Data**

Crockett, Andrew.
  Strengthening the international monetary system.

  (Occasional paper, ISSN 0251-6365 ; no. 50)
  "February 1987."
  1. International finance. 2. Foreign exchange problem.
3. Monetary policy. I. Goldstein, Morris, 1944–
II. International Monetary Fund. III. Title. IV. Series:
Occasional paper (International Monetary Fund) ; no. 50.
HG3881.C694  1987        332.4'5         86-33750
ISBN 0-939934-76-0

Price: US$7.50
(US$4.50 university libraries, faculty members, and students)

Address orders to:
External Relations Department, Publications Unit
International Monetary Fund, Washington, D.C. 20431

# Contents

|  |  | Page |
|---|---|---|
| **Prefatory Note** | | vii |
| **I** | **The System of Floating Exchange Rates: Review and Assessment** | 1 |
| | Perceived Weaknesses of Present System | 2 |
| |    Short-Run Volatility | 2 |
| |    Large and Persistent Misalignments of Real Exchange Rates | 3 |
| |    Lack of Discipline and Coordination in Macroeconomic Policies | 6 |
| | Perceived Strengths of Present System | 7 |
| |    Promotion of External Payments Adjustment | 7 |
| |    Insulation from Inflation Abroad | 8 |
| |    Independence and Effectiveness of Domestic Monetary Policy | 9 |
| |    Resilience of Present System | 10 |
| | Proposals for Improving Exchange Rate Stability | 11 |
| |    Target Zones for Exchange Rates of Major Currencies | 12 |
| |    Objective Indicators | 15 |
| |    Improvements Within Existing Institutional Setting | 17 |
| **II** | **Surveillance Over Exchange Rate Policies** | 21 |
| | Guidelines for Floating, 1974 | 22 |
| | 1977 Document | 23 |
| |    Global Economic Environment, 1977 | 23 |
| |    Lessons of Early Experience With Floating | 24 |
| |    Implications for Surveillance | 24 |
| | Exchange Rate System Since 1977 | 25 |
| |    Changing Policy Issues | 25 |
| |    Weaknesses in Working of Exchange Rate System | 26 |
| |    Implications for Surveillance Principles | 27 |
| | Possible Modifications in Surveillance | 28 |
| |    Some Objectives | 28 |
| |    General Principles | 29 |
| |    Principles for Guidance of Members' Exchange Rate Policies | 29 |
| |    Principles of Fund Surveillance Over Exchange Rate Policies | 32 |
| |    Procedures | 33 |
| **III** | **Indicators of Policies and Economic Performance** | 34 |
| | Purpose of Indicators | 34 |
| | An Analytical Framework | 35 |
| |    Factors Influencing Balance of Payments | 36 |
| |    Criteria for Assessing Sustainability of Payments Balances | 37 |
| | Types of Economic Indicator: Uses, Scope, and Limitations | 37 |
| |    Indicators of Economic Performance | 37 |
| |    Indicators of Economic Policy | 39 |
| |    Indicators of Intermediate Variables | 42 |
| | Concluding Observations | 42 |

CONTENTS

| | **APPENDIX** | Page |
|---|---|---|
| I | **Report of the Deputies of the Group of Ten: The Functioning of the International Monetary System** | **44** |
| | Chapter I:   Introduction | 44 |
| | Chapter II:   The Functioning of Floating Exchange Rates | 44 |
| |   General Considerations | 44 |
| |   Assessment of Floating Exchange Rates | 45 |
| |   Proposals to Improve Exchange Rate Stability | 46 |
| | Chapter III:   Strengthening International Surveillance | 48 |
| |   General Considerations | 48 |
| |   Proposals to Strengthen Surveillance | 48 |
| |   Article IV Surveillance | 49 |
| |   Multilateral Surveillance | 50 |
| | Chapter IV:   The Management of International Liquidity | 51 |
| |   General Considerations | 51 |
| |   Proposals Concerning International Liquidity | 52 |
| |   Present and Future Role of the SDR | 52 |
| | Chapter V:   The Role of the IMF | 54 |
| |   General Considerations | 54 |
| |   Strengthening the Role of the IMF | 55 |
| |   IMF/IBRD Cooperation | 55 |
| | Chapter VI:   Summary and Conclusions | 56 |
| |   General Considerations | 56 |
| |   The Exchange Rate System | 56 |
| |   Surveillance | 57 |
| |   International Liquidity | 58 |
| |   The Role of the IMF | 59 |
| II | **Report of the Deputies of the Group of Twenty-Four:   The Functioning and Improvement of the International Monetary System** | **60** |
| | Chapter I:   Summary of Recommendations | 60 |
| |   The Functioning of the Present Exchange Rate System | 60 |
| |   Surveillance | 60 |
| |   Management of International Liquidity and the SDR | 61 |
| |   Role of the IMF | 62 |
| |   The Debt Problem and Transfer of Resources | 63 |
| |   Follow-Up Action | 64 |
| | Chapter II:   Introduction | 64 |
| | Chapter III:   An Overview of the International Economic Situation | 65 |
| | Chapter IV:   The Functioning of the Present Exchange Rate System | 66 |
| |   The Experience with Floating Rates | 66 |
| |   Proposals for Improving Exchange Rate Stability | 67 |
| | Chapter V:   Surveillance | 68 |
| |   The Objectives of Surveillance | 68 |
| |   The Analytical Basis of Surveillance | 69 |
| |   Pressures to Make Surveillance Effective | 69 |
| |   Enhanced Surveillance | 70 |
| | Chapter VI:   Management of International Liquidity and the SDR | 70 |
| |   Management of International Liquidity | 70 |
| |   The SDR | 71 |

|  |  | Page |
|---|---|---|
| | Chapter VII: Role of the IMF | 73 |
| | Transitory Balance of Payments Problems | 73 |
| | Persistent Imbalances Requiring Adjustment | 74 |
| | Need for Concessionality in IMF Lending | 75 |
| | The Volume of IMF Resources | 75 |
| | Enlarged Access Policy and Access Limits | 76 |
| | IMF/IBRD Collaboration | 76 |
| | The Decision-Making Process | 77 |
| | Chapter VIII: The Debt Problem and Transfer of Resources | 77 |
| | Problems Relating to External Debt | 78 |
| | Trade and Finance | 78 |
| | Transfer of Resources to Developing Countries | 79 |
| **III** | **Executive Board Decisions on Surveillance Over Exchange Rate Policies** | **80** |
| | 1977 Decision and Document | 80 |
| | 1979 Decision | 82 |
| **References** | | **83** |

---

The following symbols have been used throughout this paper:

. . . to indicate that data are not available;

— to indicate that the figure is zero or less than half the final digit shown, or that the time does not exist;

– between years or months (e.g., 1984–85 or January–June) to indicate the years or months covered, including the beginning and ending years or months;

/ between years (e.g., 1985/86) to indicate a crop or fiscal (financial) year.

"Billion" means a thousand million.

Minor discrepancies between constituent figures and totals are due to rounding.

# Prefatory Note

*Strengthening the International Monetary System: Exchange Rates, Surveillance, and Objective Indicators* comprises three papers written by staff members of the Fund's Research Department on issues arising out of the reports on the international monetary system prepared in 1985 by the Group of Ten (representing the industrial countries participating in the General Arrangements to Borrow) and the intergovernmental Group of Twenty-Four on International Monetary Affairs. These two reports, which appear as appendices to this volume, were transmitted to the Interim Committee of the Fund's Board of Governors and were subsequently discussed by the Fund's Executive Board in early 1986. The views in the papers published here are the authors' own and do not necessarily reflect those of the Executive Directors or member authorities.

Chapter 1, on the system of floating exchange rates, is by Morris Goldstein, and Chapters II and III on surveillance and indicators are by Andrew Crockett. The publication was edited in the External Relations Department by Joslin Landell-Mills.

It is to be noted that the term "country" used in this document does not, in all cases, refer to a territorial entity that is a state as understood by international law and practice. The term also covers some territorial entities that are not states, but for which statistical data are maintained and provided internationally on a separate independent basis.

# I The System of Floating Exchange Rates: Review and Assessment

At its meeting in Seoul on October 6–7, 1985, the Interim Committee of the Board of Governors of the International Monetary Fund requested the Fund's Executive Board "... to study the issues raised in these reports [the reports on the international monetary system presented by the Group of Ten and the Group of Twenty-Four] with a view to facilitating a substantive consideration by the Committee at its next meeting." [1] This chapter, as part of the response to that request, discusses issues directly related to the functioning and improvement of the exchange rate system.

The Reports of the Group of Ten and the Group of Twenty-Four share some important conclusions on the exchange rate system.[2] In brief, both reports conclude that the functioning of the present system of floating exchange rates needs to be improved; that the variability of exchange rates, both in the short run and in the long run, has been a source of concern; that unsound and inconsistent policies, and related divergences in economic performance among major industrial countries, have been central elements in the observed volatility and misalignments of key currency exchange rates; that surveillance is crucial for an orderly international monetary and financial system and is a basic tool for promoting convergence of economic performances toward sustainable noninflationary growth; that while exchange market intervention can play a useful supplementary or complementary role, it cannot be the primary instrument for achieving exchange rate stability; and finally, that a return to a rigid par value system is neither desirable nor feasible at the present time.

In some other respects, however, the two Reports are quite far apart in their diagnosis of and proposed remedies for the present exchange rate system. The Group of Ten Report concludes that "... the fundamental approach of the Articles of Agreement remains valid;" [3] that the present system of floating rates has shown "valuable strengths" [4] (as well as weaknesses); and that "... the key elements ... require no major institutional change." [5] In contrast, the Group of Twenty-Four Report concludes that "the experience with the present exchange rate system has not been satisfactory;" [6] that "volatility and misalignment of exchange rates have especially hurt the developing countries;" [7] and that "... a mechanism has to be devised to enforce policy coordination among the major industrial countries." [8] On the issue of target zones for exchange rates of major currencies, the gulf was also wide. The majority of Deputies in the Group of Ten Report considered the adoption of target zones "... undesirable and in any case impractical in present circumstances" [9] (some Deputies, however, did think that the proposal could have merits and suggested further exploration of its technical aspects at an appropriate time). In contrast, the Group of Twenty-Four Report expressed the view that target zones "... could help achieve the objective of exchange rate stability and a sustainable pattern of payments balances"; [10] it also concluded that the proposal needed to be further studied and pursued to gain general acceptance. Yet another difference is that the Group of Twenty-Four Report envisages a role for a set of

---

[1] "Communiqué of the Interim Committee of the Board of Governors of the International Monetary Fund," paragraph 10, International Monetary Fund, Press Release No. 85/33, October 7, 1985.

[2] "The Functioning of the International Monetary System: A Report to the Ministers and Governors by the Deputies of the Group of Ten," June 1985, published in *IMF Survey, Supplement on the Fund* (Washington), Vol. 14 (July 1985). "The Functioning and Improvement of the International Monetary System: Report of the Deputies of the Group of Twenty-Four," August 1985, published in the *IMF Survey, Supplement on the Fund* (Washington), Vol. 14 (September 1985). The reports are reproduced in the Appendix and are referred to in this paper as the Group of Ten Report and the Group of Twenty-Four Report.

[3] Group of Ten Report, paragraph 97.
[4] Group of Ten Report, paragraph 14.
[5] Group of Ten Report, paragraph 97.
[6] Group of Twenty-Four Report, paragraph 2.
[7] Group of Twenty-Four Report, paragraph 3.
[8] Group of Twenty-Four Report, paragraph 5.
[9] Group of Ten Report, paragraph 32.
[10] Group of Twenty-Four Report, paragraph 5.

"objective indicators or targets" [11] in the conduct of multilateral surveillance while the Group of Ten Report emphasizes "... enhanced dialogue and persuasion through peer pressure." [12]

Drawing on the analysis in both Reports, as well as on earlier work done inside and outside the Fund, this chapter identifies and discusses issues and proposals for improving the functioning of the exchange rate system. The aim is to identify areas of agreement and to discuss points of contention—not to advocate any particular proposal.

The rest of the chapter is organized as follows. The next section discusses several perceived weaknesses of the present exchange rate system, namely: the high short-run volatility of exchange rates; the large and persistent misalignments of real exchange rates; and the lack of discipline and coordination in the conduct of macroeconomic policy in the major industrial countries. The third section turns to the perceived strengths of the present system. Here, the contribution of exchange rate flexibility to external payments adjustment, to insulation from shocks abroad, to the independence and effectiveness of domestic monetary policy, and to the maintenance of an open trade and payments system—are all considered. These perceived weaknesses and strengths of the present system are those given most attention in the two Reports. The final section addresses specific proposals for improving the functioning of the existing system. Three types of proposals are examined: the adoption of "target zones" for key-currency exchange rates; the introduction of "objective indicators" or quantitative targets for macroeconomic outcomes and policies into multilateral (Fund) surveillance; and more intensive use of consultative and judgmental mechanisms, within the existing institutional setting, to enhance the appropriateness and mutual compatibility of policies. (The proposals analyzed are those specifically presented in the Group of Ten and Group of Twenty-Four Reports.)

The scope of the paper has been conditioned by three considerations. First, although the focus of the paper is on the functioning and improvement of the exchange rate system, it is not appropriate to deny the interconnections between the exchange rate system and other features of the international monetary system. This is especially true for the interrelationship between the exchange rate system and surveillance.[13] For example, any changes in the operation of the exchange rate system, be they changes in exchange arrangements or improvements to policy coordination, would have to be implemented through the surveillance process. At the same time, proposals for strengthening surveillance, both at the bilateral and multilateral levels, are integral elements of most proposals for improving the functioning of the exchange rate system. The paper therefore discusses on a rather broad level the rationale for, and implications of, changes in surveillance for the operation of the exchange rate system. An in-depth treatment of surveillance issues appears in the next chapter.

Second, in discussing proposals for improving exchange rate stability, the emphasis is on the major industrial countries. This follows the view, given expression in both the Reports, that the policies and exchange rates of the major industrial countries exert the most significant impact on the functioning of the international monetary system as a whole. None of this denies, of course, either the importance of maintaining realistic exchange rates in all countries, or the desirability of an exchange rate system that adequately meets the needs of smaller industrial countries and of developing countries. Third, although this paper is organized around the issues and proposals raised in the Reports, it also considers views, evidence, and proposals on the exchange rate system from other sources. For these reasons, terms such as "proponents," "supporters," or "opponents" should not necessarily be associated with the Group of Ten and Group of Twenty-Four Reports unless specifically indicated.

## Perceived Weaknesses of Present System

Although the present system of floating exchange rates has been criticized on many counts, most of these criticisms can be grouped under the following three headings: the high short-run volatility of exchange rates; the large and persistent misalignments of real exchange rates; and lack of discipline and coordination in the conduct of macroeconomic policy in major industrial countries. Each of these criticisms, or perceived weaknesses, can be examined in turn.

### Short-Run Volatility

Prior to the advent of floating rates, some of its supporters anticipated that stabilizing speculation would

---

[11] Group of Twenty-Four Report, paragraph 78.
[12] Group of Ten Report, paragraph 38.
[13] Another potential area of interconnection is that between the exchange rate system and international liquidity. For example, proposals for liberalization of capital markets or for greater use of official intervention in exchange markets cannot be divorced from questions concerning the quantity and composition of international reserves. Still, the present study makes the assumption that many issues in the evaluation of the exchange rate system can be better discussed within the bounds of existing reserve and liquidity arrangements.

smooth exchange rate movements and prevent an abrupt increase in variability. Thirteen years of experience have proved otherwise. Whether measured in bilateral or effective terms, nominal or real terms, the short-run variability of exchange rates has been much greater during the period of floating rates than under the Bretton Woods system. A representative calculation is that the short-term (monthly or quarterly) variability of nominal exchange rates for the seven major currencies was about six times greater under floating rates than during the last decade of adjustable par values (International Monetary Fund (1984a)). In addition, there has not been a sustained tendency for exchange rate variability to decline over time. Finally, and of interest for linking exchange rate variability to exchange rate uncertainty, most exchange rate changes under floating rates have been unexpected (as revealed by market indicators of expected exchange rates, such as forward rates).

Critics of floating exchange rates contend that one of the main reasons why rates have been so volatile is that market participants lack an anchor for medium-term exchange rate expectations. Without such an anchor, short-term events (be they news, rumors, or shifts in policy) induce large revisions of expectations about future exchange rates, which in turn induce large changes in current rates. Without an anchor, too, the risks of self-fulfilling destabilizing speculation (such as bandwagon effects or speculative bubbles) are increased.

This short-run variability, or volatility, of exchange rates is said to be costly because its associated uncertainty reduces the volume of trade and investment.[14] These costs are claimed to be especially heavy for developing countries which do not have well-developed financial markets, particularly forward cover arrangements.[15]

The high short-term volatility of exchange rates under floating is not in dispute. What is contentious is the proper yardstick for evaluating that volatility and the costs associated with it. Defenders of the present system make the following points.

First, while the variability of nominal exchange rates has been higher than the variability of the ratio of national price levels, it has been lower than that for other asset prices (such as national stock market prices, changes in commodity prices, or changes in interest rates).[16] This higher variability of exchange rates is said to reflect the fact that exchange rates are jumpy, forward-looking auction prices that anticipate future events, whereas prices and wages are sticky, backward-looking administered prices that largely reflect past contractual commitments. Hence, some greater variability in exchange rates is to be expected. The fact that all asset prices have been so variable during the floating rate period is often explained by the accompanying turbulence in the global economic and political environment.[17]

Second, and probably more challenging, the defenders argue that there is little evidence that short-run exchange rate volatility has been very costly in either a relative or absolute sense. The question of relative costs hinges on which markets are best able to handle disturbances. The point is that if exchange rates were more rigid, then disturbances would be transferred to goods or labor markets, or would induce limitations on trade and capital movements, both of which might be more costly than the exchange rate movements themselves. As to the absolute cost, the defenders of the present system note that a large body of econometric work has produced only sporadic evidence of a link between measures of exchange rate volatility and the volume of international trade (International Monetary Fund (1984a)). It is also argued that the development of various hedging techniques and futures markets has increased the ability of market participants to both reduce their exposure to risk and to purchase relatively low-cost insurance against it.[18]

## Large and Persistent Misalignments of Real Exchange Rates

A second indictment of the present system is that real exchange rates of major currencies have been subject to large and persistent misalignments. The term misalignment is commonly interpreted as a deviation of the actual real exchange rate from its "equilibrium" level.

In practice, misalignment has usually been estimated by, or inferred from, three types of calculations. First, it can be calculated as the cumulative departure of the nominal exchange rate from the path implied by purchasing power parity. This is equivalent to calculating the deviation of the current real exchange rate from

---

[14] "It [volatility of exchange rates] has discouraged investment and trade by adding to financial risks for investors and traders," Group of Twenty-Four Report, paragraph 61.

[15] "Exporters and importers in these countries [developing countries] are exposed to high exchange risks in the absence of well-developed financial markets, especially forward cover arrangements. The destabilizing uncertainties of floating rates have increased the reserve and capital needs of developing countries from the levels which would otherwise exist," Group of Twenty-Four Report, paragraph 63.

[16] Bergstrand (1983).

[17] Frenkel and Mussa (1980).

[18] "... Foreign exchange markets appear to have developed effective hedging techniques available to most operators to reduce the risks associated with exchange rate volatility, generally at comparatively little cost," Group of Ten Report, paragraph 16.

its level in some "equilibrium" base period. Second, misalignment is sometimes inferred from the sheer size of real exchange rate movements themselves. The implicit assumption here is that the equilibrium real exchange rate will change only gradually in response to structural changes in competitiveness and comparative advantage. The third method is to compute misalignment as the deviation of the real exchange rate from the level that would yield an equilibrium in the balance of payments (given anticipated macroeconomic policies over the following two to three years). The equilibrium balance of payments, in turn, is defined as an "underlying" current account balance equal to "normal" net capital flows. In addition, this equality must be achieved without resort to either undesirable levels of unemployment, or "undue" restrictions on trade, or "special" incentives to incoming or outgoing capital.[19]

As representative (albeit dramatic) examples of such calculations, one might offer the following: in the second quarter of 1985, the real effective exchange rate of the U.S. dollar was over 50 percent above the level implied by purchasing power parity (using 1980 as the base);[20] between 1975 and 1976, the real effective exchange rate of the pound sterling fell by 20 percent, only to rise by nearly 75 percent between 1976 and 1981; and using an "underlying balance" approach to calculating the equilibrium real exchange rate, one recent study estimated that the misalignments of the U.S. dollar and the Japanese yen at end-1984 were 39 percent and 19 percent, respectively.[21]

Although it was originally thought that real exchange rate movements under floating rates would be dominated by the gradual changes in competitiveness needed to restore current account equilibria, it is now recognized that large capital flows, often stimulated by short-term considerations, have usually been the predominant force.[22] These capital flows, in turn, have been influenced by inter-country differences in interest rates that have reflected different stances and mixes of monetary and fiscal policy and by changes in expectations about the future course of these policies and their impact on future interest rates and future exchange rates. In addition, rigidities in goods and labor markets have meant that nominal exchange rates have borne the brunt of the adjustment, often "overshooting" their long-term values, to compensate for the stickiness of nominal wages and prices in the short run.

Such misalignments in the real exchange rates among major currencies have been costly, so it is argued, because: (1) they distort resource allocation and generate "boom and bust" cycles in the tradable goods sector that leave unemployment in their wake; and (2) because they encourage protectionism, as firms and governments attempt to overrule the unjust verdict of the market place by turning to administrative solutions.[23]

By now, there is widespread agreement that the floating rate era has been marked by cases of serious misalignment. Not so clear are the extent of these misalignments, their cost, and perhaps most of all, whether alternative exchange rate systems could eliminate or reduce them. In this connection, defenders of the present system offer the following arguments.

First, not all of the large swings in real exchange rates that have been observed over the past thirteen years represent misalignment. Some of it represents desirable adjustments to changes in real economic conditions, such as continuing inter-country differences in labor productivity, permanent changes in the terms of trade (sometimes associated with discovery of, or large price changes in, natural resources), permanent shifts in savings-investment relationships across countries, or safe-haven considerations. For example, a good portion of the appreciation of sterling between 1977 and 1981 could be represented as an equilibrium response to the United Kingdom's enhanced status as an oil exporter.[24] Even under a system of pegged exchange rates, such changes would call for changes in real equilibrium exchange rates. Under that regime, these changes would occur primarily via changes in national price levels, aided by occasional changes in parities. Under floating rates, the required changes in relative prices occur primarily via changes in nominal exchange rates and they happen more quickly. But, according to defenders of the present system, this need not imply that the latter form of adjustment is inferior to the former.

---

[19] This definition is similar to those found in Nurkse (1945), International Monetary Fund (1970), and the Group of Twenty-Four Report, paragraph 69.

[20] The real effective exchange rate used for these calculations is the relative normalized unit labor cost in manufacturing.

[21] Williamson (1985).

[22] ". . . exchange rate determination has been increasingly influenced by conditions in capital markets, including relative interest rates and expectations regarding the impact of national policies and current and future economic performance," Group of Ten Report, paragraph 18. "Much of the medium-term movement in real exchange rates reflects not the changing pattern of competitiveness but rather the result of differences in fiscal and monetary policies. . . ," Group of Twenty-Four Report, paragraph 62.

[23] "Misalignment inevitably produces either idle resources or wasteful shifts back and forth between tradables and nontradables. It becomes a potent source of pressures for protectionism," Group of Twenty-Four Report, paragraph 62.

[24] See, for example, Bond and Knobl (1982).

Second, although misalignment may not be so difficult to define, it can be very difficult to measure when concepts like "normal" capital flows, "undue" restrictions on trade, "special" incentives to incoming or outgoing capital, "cyclically-adjusted" current accounts, and "anticipated" macroeconomic policies have to be estimated. For example, a country that is a "normal" net capital exporter under one set of macroeconomic policies, tax considerations, and political events abroad may become a normal net capital importer under others. For example, if, say, one third of the recent private net capital inflow into the United States was regarded as "normal" (reflecting attractive perceived investment opportunities and a relatively low domestic savings rate), then estimates of the current misalignment of the U.S. dollar would be considerably below estimates that assume a normal net capital flow of zero for the United States. Yet some would argue that the theory and evidence for preferring the latter assumption to the former are weak. An additional complicating factor is the existence of a large statistical discrepancy in world balance of payments accounts, whose geographical attribution is highly uncertain.

Supporters of the present system acknowledge that misalignments of key currencies carry costs but suggest caution in identifying misalignments as primary factors in explaining both the recent weakness of manufacturing employment in the United States and the resurgence of protectionist pressures in major industrial countries as a group.

While it is true, for example, that the ratio of manufacturing employment to total nonagricultural employment in the United States declined sharply over the 1979–83 period, it also declined in 1969–71 against the background of a depreciating real exchange rate for the dollar; in fact, it has declined in all periods of recession since 1969. Further, this ratio increased in 1984 when the real exchange rate of the dollar was appreciating sharply. Likewise, the same ratio rose in the Federal Republic of Germany during 1976–79 when the deutsche mark was appreciating, and fell during 1980–83 when the deutsche mark was depreciating. In Japan, the manufacturing employment ratio has been flat since 1978, despite a strong real appreciation of the yen from 1982–84.[25] All of this suggests that one has to specify the type of disturbance moving the real exchange rate before one can predict the link between the real exchange rate and the sectoral allocation of resources. As Obstfeld (1985) points out, an increase in foreign demand for domestic manufactures may cause both a currency appreciation and an expansion in manufacturing employment, whereas a shift to restrictive monetary policy will induce both currency appreciation and contraction in manufacturing employment.

Supporters of the present system also argue that exchange rate misalignment is only one of several important factors explaining the rising tide of protectionism. They note, for example, that many of the current protectionist measures or proposals have been sector oriented or country specific and have been influenced by long-lasting shifts in competitiveness arising from factors other than exchange rate shifts. In clothing and textiles, for example, restrictions have been directed against developing countries with a comparative cost advantage and restrictions have become progressively more severe over a quarter of a century, almost irrespective of changes in exchange rates. Nor does the degree of protection of the agricultural sector and of the steel sector correlate well with exchange rate movements. More generally, it can be argued that pressures for protection will be greater not only when a country's exchange rate is overvalued but also, inter alia: the higher and more rapidly increasing is its unemployment rate, the smaller and less generous are its existing trade adjustment programs, the higher is its ratio of imports to consumption, the larger is employment in import-competing industries, and the higher is the level of general government intervention.[26]

Finally, defenders of the present system recall that misalignment and overshooting of the exchange rates among the major currencies were by no means unknown during the Bretton Woods era, especially in its later years.[27] For example, the effective real exchange rate of the dollar depreciated by 28 percent from 1969–73. Similarly, if a currency had long been overvalued under the Bretton Woods system, and the authorities at last decided on a devaluation, they usually chose a new parity which undervalued the currency at the current level of prices. One common justification for such excessive devaluation was that it was necessary to replenish the level of reserves which had become unduly low during the period of overvaluation.[28] In short, defenders argue that the current system ought not to be compared to some unobservable textbook ideal but rather to the also-flawed real-world alternatives.

---

[25] All these figures on manufacturing employment are drawn from Obstfeld (1985).

[26] Bergsten and Williamson (1983).

[27] Dunn (1973) and Makin (1974) provide evidence of the trade and investment distortions created by misaligned real exchange rates during the Bretton Woods era.

[28] Machlup (1979).

## Lack of Discipline and Coordination in Macroeconomic Policies

The third criticism of the present exchange rate system is that it has not promoted discipline and coordination in the conduct of macroeconomic policy. Indeed, this is probably the single most damaging charge because short-term volatility and longer-term misalignments are both widely regarded as manifestations of this failure to get underlying monetary and fiscal policies "right." [29]

Under floating exchange rates, one can expect: (1) the current exchange rate to be heavily influenced by the expected future exchange rate; and (2) the expected future exchange rate to be heavily influenced by expected future macroeconomic policies. Since instability in current policies generates uncertainty about future policies, it is clear why disciplined and consistent policies are judged to be a sine qua non for greater stability in exchange rates.

Evidence of a lack of discipline and coordination in macroeconomic policy over the past thirteen years is not hard to find. Critics of the present system point to, inter alia, the near-doubling of average industrial-country inflation rates between 1963–72 and 1973–85 (from 4.2 percent to 7.6 percent) and to the tripling of the average ratio of industrial country (central) government fiscal deficits to gross national product (GNP) over the same period (from 1.2 percent to 3.7 percent). They also note that there have been frequent occurrences of large changes in monetary and fiscal policies being made in a seemingly independent fashion, with too little thought given to their international repercussions. They point in particular to the 1979–83 period when the stance and mix of policies in the major industrial countries (particularly the heavy reliance on monetary restraint) produced historically high real interest rates, low commodity prices, and sluggish economic activity with adverse "spillover" effects for developing countries' debt service, export earnings, and growth performance.[30] Finally, critics note that efforts at better coordination during the floating rate period have not produced binding agreements on either monetary and fiscal policies or on exchange rates.

The view that discipline and coordination of macroeconomic policies in industrial countries needs to be improved is now widely accepted. The main point at issue is what contribution the exchange rate system can make toward achieving that objective. Critics of the present system maintain that the obligation to defend the parity in a fixed rate system obliges the more inflationary countries to discipline themselves in order to avoid repeated (and politically costly) realignments. On the other hand, supporters of the present system offer the following arguments.

First, experience suggests to them that greater fixity of exchange rates is neither necessary nor sufficient for enforcing discipline on macroeconomic policy. They note, for example, that the deceleration in growth rates of narrow and broad money that took place in most of the major industrial countries in 1979–82 (in the face of high unemployment) was accomplished without exchange rate targets; hence, greater fixity of exchange rates is not "necessary" for anti-inflationary discipline. Similarly, even during the Bretton Woods era, there were too many cases of exchange rate targets giving way to employment targets when the two came into conflict to believe that greater fixity of exchange rates is "sufficient." In fact, they would say that history is more kind to the proposition that the exchange rate regime is determined by the degree and inter-country dispersion of discipline in macroeconomic policies than to the reverse line of causation.

Second, some observers argue that the exchange rate regime does not necessarily have a comparative advantage over other institutional mechanisms for imposing discipline on national authorities. For example, if greater discipline in monetary policy is sought, then pre-announced money supply rules, or even various types of commodity standards are alternative roads to making a nonaccommodation strategy more credible. As regards discipline for fiscal policy, fixed rates may, so the argument goes, be even less effective than flexible rates. This is because (under fixed rates) an expansionary fiscal policy that is not monetized draws in capital from abroad and leads to an increase in foreign exchange reserves; hence, reserve movements impose no discipline. In contrast, expansionary fiscal policy (with tight monetary policy) under flexible rates induces currency appreciation that may in turn lead to political pressure from the traded goods sector for fiscal restraint.[31] And if discipline against inflation is the primary concern, measures that

---

[29] "It [the present exchange rate system] has not prevented inadequate policies and divergent economic performance which have contributed to a high degree of short-term volatility of nominal exchange rates and to large medium-term movements in real exchange rates," Group of Ten Report, paragraph 5. "This [improved functioning of the exchange rate system] implies greater effort on the part of the developed countries to achieve a substantial degree of discipline and coordination in the conduct of their national policies," Group of Twenty-Four Report, paragraph 65.

[30] "In the recent past, their [industrial countries] uncoordinated attempts to disinflate led to excessive emphasis being given to monetary restriction relative to other instruments. The result was a halting process of recovery with high real interest rates and low commodity prices having particularly adverse effects on the developing countries," Group of Twenty-Four Report, paragraph 72.

[31] An alternative point of view, inspired by the recent experience of the United States, is that strains in the traded goods sector tend to lead to protectionist pressures more than to fiscal restraint.

substitute rules for discretion in determining the world money stock, or that put a tax on inflationary wage settlements (such as tax-based incomes policy) may represent more direct constraints.

Third, although trying to describe the "counterfactual" is always a speculative exercise, some have argued that a fixed exchange rate between the United States and the rest of the Organization for Economic Cooperation and Development (OECD) was not likely to have prevented either the recent real appreciation of the U.S. dollar or its international effects.[32] The argument here is that fixed rates and fiscal expansion in the United States would still have meant relatively high U.S. interest rates and a large net capital inflow. The capital inflow in turn would have lowered foreign money supplies and (unless sterilized) increased the U.S. money supply. The effects of these money supply changes would thus have been to raise U.S. prices relative to those abroad. One would still get a real appreciation of the U.S. dollar, but this time operating mainly via national price levels rather than via the nominal exchange rate. Alternatively, attempts to prevent these money supply changes from taking place under fixed rates (via capital controls or sterilization operations) would only lead to a higher level of interest rates and would remove, so the argument goes, the inflationary pressure for a fiscal reversal. The alleged moral of this scenario is that fiscal reform rather than exchange rate reform is the necessary ingredient for preventing misalignment and its effects.

Fourth, supporters of the present system caution that there are "natural" limits to coordination of policies, whatever the exchange rate regime. Exchange rates and interest rates are by their very nature "competitive" in the sense that one country's gain is frequently the other's loss. Also, the compromise of growth and inflation objectives at the national level often leaves little room for further compromise on demand policies at the international level.[33] Given these limits, past efforts at coordination (such as the U.S. dollar support package of November 1, 1978, the agreements of the Bonn economic summit of 1978, and the September 1985 Group of Five agreement in New York on exchange rates and adjustment policies)—while perhaps still far from optimal—should, in their view, not be seen in too bad a light.

Finally, supporters of the present system are wary of comparisons between the period of floating rates and that of par values. They note that many features of the global economic environment that are important for macroeconomic performance but are not proximately related to the exchange rate regime, were also changing during the period of floating rates.[34] For example, inflation performance during the floating rate period may have been distorted by the two rounds of large oil price increases (1973–74 and 1979–80) and by the huge expansion (57 percent) in international reserves in 1970–72 associated with the collapse of the Bretton Woods system.

## Perceived Strengths of Present System

While both the Reports agree that the existing exchange rate regime has shown weaknesses, the Group of Ten emphasizes that it has also displayed some "valuable strengths." More specifically, they stress that exchange rate flexibility has made positive contributions to "external payments adjustment," to "insulation of domestic price levels from inflation abroad," and to "the pursuit of sound monetary policies geared more directly to domestic conditions."[35] Finally, they doubt whether any less flexible system could have survived the strains of the past decade without increased reliance on restrictions on trade and capital flows. Each of these perceived strengths is discussed in this section.

### Promotion of External Payments Adjustment

Although it has perhaps not provided all that was hoped for prior to the advent of floating rates, supporters of the present system maintain that exchange rate flexibility has made a positive contribution to external payments adjustment on at least three counts.

First, the extent of payments adjustment in the floating rate period (1973–85) has been somewhat better than that during the last decade of adjustable par values (1963–72), at least for the seven largest industrial countries—and this despite the occurrence of some unusually large external shocks during the floating rate period (including the two large increases in world oil prices in 1973–74 and 1979–80). Simple measures of payments imbalances, such as the ratio of current account balances alone to GNP or the ratio of current accounts plus normal capital flows to GNP, show smaller mean imbalances and less persistence (that is,

---

[32] See, for example, Obstfeld (1985).
[33] See Polak (1981) for an expansion of both these points.

[34] "It would be misleading to draw definite conclusions on the merits and demerits of the present system merely by comparing economic performance in the period of floating with that recorded under the par value system. Conditions during the floating rate period have been different in too many respects to allow such a comparison to be meaningful," Group of Ten Report, paragraph 13.
[35] Group of Ten Report, paragraph 14.

serial correlation), on average, for 1973–85 than for 1963–72.

Second, the symmetry of adjustment is alleged to have improved. Recall that two well-known charges against the Bretton Woods system were: that surplus countries were subject to a much weaker discipline than deficit countries; and that reserve centers, particularly the United States, had an unwarranted privilege because they could finance payments deficits by liability as opposed to asset settlement. Both of these asymmetries are said to have been much reduced under floating: there is no evidence (among industrial countries) that mean payments imbalances are larger or more persistent for surplus countries, and the privilege (some would say dangers) of liability settlement has since been extended to many countries, including developing ones.

Third, exchange rate flexibility has, according to its proponents, reduced the cost of adjustment. The argument here is that when exchange rates are less flexible, the burden of adjustment falls more on expenditure-reducing measures and less on expenditure-switching ones, with heavier costs in terms of real output and employment.[36] They further point out that econometric studies indicate that exchange rate depreciation is likely to be effective in improving the trade balance in the medium to long term, and that there is no evidence that price elasticities for traded goods have declined since the onset of floating rates.[37]

The contribution of exchange rate flexibility to external payments adjustment is still a matter of some dispute. Critics of the present system offer the following counter-arguments.

On the extent of external adjustment, they note that current account performance of some large industrial countries has been anything but satisfactory over the past three years; that current account performance for the smaller industrial countries has been significantly worse, on average, during 1973–84 than during the last ten years of Bretton Woods; and that reversal of current account imbalances, even for the larger industrial countries, has typically taken an extremely long time (on the order of three to seven years).[38] In addition, they mention that more sophisticated measures of equilibrium payments balances suggest that there have been many instances during the floating rate period of unsustainable or undesirable payments outcomes.[39] In short, the extent of external payments adjustment under floating rates may have been marginally better on average than during the Bretton Woods period but it was far from satisfactory.

The symmetry of external adjustment between surplus and deficit countries may have improved under floating rates, but critics contend that some asymmetries have become worse. In particular, the burden of external adjustment is alleged to fall much harder now on the developing than on the industrial countries.[40] Further, it could be argued that within the industrial-country group, external adjustment has been least effective in the very countries with the most substantial spillover effects on the world economy. Also, whereas the United States is admittedly no longer the only country to enjoy the privilege of liability settlement, some might argue that it now enjoys a new unwarranted privilege—namely, to finance an unusually large part of its fiscal deficit with the rest of the world's savings.

Finally, while exchange rate changes may well improve the current account in the medium to long-term, critics note that there can be substantial "J-curve" effects in the short to medium term. Further, even in the long term, exchange rate changes will not be an equally effective instrument for achieving external balance in all countries; instead, its relative effectiveness depends in good measure on the economy's structural characteristics. Specifically, both theory and empirical evidence suggest that the smaller, more open, more highly indexed economies suffer proportionately larger domestic price feedbacks and obtain less lasting relative-price advantages from exchange rate changes than do the larger, less open, and less indexed economies.[41] Therefore, the extent to which exchange rate flexibility reduces the cost of adjustment is not the same for everybody.[42]

## Insulation from Inflation Abroad

Prior to the actual experience with floating exchange rates, it was thought by many that floating exchange rates would be premier insulators against a whole

---

[36] An implicit assumption in this argument is that it is more difficult to alter the relative price of tradables in the presence of a relatively rigid nominal exchange rate.

[37] International Monetary Fund (1984a) and Goldstein and Khan (1985).

[38] See International Monetary Fund (1984c) and Shafer and Loopesko (1983).

[39] See International Monetary Fund (1984b), (1984c), and Williamson (1985).

[40] "It [the surveillance function of the IMF] has so far been largely ineffective on major industrial countries, resulting in asymmetry in the international adjustment process, the burden of which has fallen disproportionately on developing countries," Group of Twenty-Four Report, paragraph 9.

[41] See Goldstein and Khan, 1985.

[42] "It [exchange rate depreciation] . . . could also . . . stimulate cost inflation. . . . It is much less useful in countries that have to rely on exports of traditional agricultural and mineral commodities. . . ," Group of Twenty-Four Report, paragraph 87. ". . . the degree of exchange rate stability deemed appropriate differs from country to country," Group of Ten Report, paragraph 11.

range of foreign disturbances. The last thirteen years have shattered that illusion. It is now widely accepted that the insulating properties of floating rates are more modest.[43] Specifically, floating rates can provide good insulation against a rise in the world price level because an appreciation of the domestic currency proportionate to the increase in foreign prices prevents wealth or relative price effects from taking place. But floating rates cannot insulate against relative price changes among different classes of traded goods because they cannot alter relative prices at that level of aggregation. Beyond that, the relative insulating properties of floating rates vis-à-vis fixed rates cannot be generalized without specifying the nature of the disturbance (monetary or real), the origin of the disturbance (domestic or foreign), what is to be insulated (real output or consumption), and who is to be insulated (the home country alone or the home and foreign country taken jointly).[44]

Having acknowledged this, defenders of the present system still emphasize that the insulation provided by floating rates against inflation abroad should not be underrated.[45] After all, it was the very inability to protect themselves from imported inflation that induced some countries to abandon the Bretton Woods system in the early 1970s.[46] Also, so long as there remains a significant risk for the future that some countries will not follow reasonable monetary and fiscal policies, it would in their view be premature to abandon the protection offered by floating rates against this risk.

Critics of the present system might reply that the dominant shocks of the 1970s and the 1980s (that is, relative price changes among different classes of traded goods such as oil, and sharp changes in interest rates) have been the very ones against which floating rates have a comparative disadvantage in insulation vis-à-vis fixed rates. In addition, they observe that available empirical evidence suggests that the international synchronization of real and monetary variables has been even higher during the period of floating rates than during the era of par values.[47] This evidence would be consistent with a greater incidence of common external shocks and common policy responses to them under floating rates but it could just as well imply greater transmission of disturbances under floating rates. Some critics of the present system would go further and conclude that because floating rates cannot provide good insulation against the representative set of foreign disturbances, the case for policy activism to combat such disturbances, including greater use of exchange market intervention, is strengthened.[48]

## Independence and Effectiveness of Domestic Monetary Policy

One reason why floating rates seemed attractive in the latter years of the par value system was that by then the incompatibility of fixed exchange rates, high international mobility of capital, and independence for domestic monetary policies had become readily apparent. This was particularly the case in the Federal Republic of Germany and Switzerland where restrictive monetary measures (taken to avoid imported inflation) brought forth an unending sequence of capital inflows, official intervention to support the U.S. dollar, and more capital inflows. Floating rates offered a way out of that dilemma. Specifically, since there would no longer be an obligation to use exchange market intervention to peg the exchange rate, exchange market pressure could take the form of exchange rate changes rather than reserve movements and the foreign component of the monetary base would be stable. In short, floating rates would allow countries to regain control over their own money supplies. A second attraction was that floating rates, at least in theory, were supposed to strengthen the output and employment effects of expansionary monetary policy via the positive effects of the induced exchange rate depreciation on the trade balance.

More than a decade later, even the supporters of the present system would probably acknowledge that the case for the independence and effectiveness of monetary policy under floating rates was exaggerated. Many of the constraints on monetary policy seem in retrospect to be as much related to the openness of national economies as to the exchange rate regime per se. These constraints show up in either a reduced ability to control the instruments of monetary policy

---

[43] "... the Deputies recognize that no exchange rate system can provide full insulation from the effects of economic policies and performance in other countries," Group of Ten Report, paragraph 22.

[44] Fiscal disturbances would be described as real disturbances in the classification presented above.

[45] "It [exchange rate flexibility] can help countries, especially the larger ones, to insulate their domestic price levels from inflation abroad...," Group of Ten Report, paragraph 14.

[46] A counter-argument of the supporters of the Bretton Woods system is that the collapse of that system reflected not any intrinsic design flaws but rather faulty implementation. In particular, the system was undermined by "excessive" fixity in nominal exchange rates that produced large misalignments in key-currency real exchange rates.

[47] See Swoboda (1983) and International Monetary Fund (1984c).

[48] "Intervention ... could be used on a meaningful scale, without confining it to 'leaning against the wind,' towards the end of exchange rate stability, as a complementary measure to other policies, and sometimes in coordination with other countries," Group of Twenty-Four Report, paragraph 67.

(the nominal money supply under fixed rates), or a reduced ability to control some of the targets of monetary policy (the level of real output), or an increased caution in the use of monetary policy because of potentially dangerous effects on expectations.

Still, supporters of the present system maintain that floating rates have been instrumental in facilitating "... the pursuit of sound monetary policies geared more directly to domestic conditions." [49] They are credited with having increased countries' control over their own money supplies without resort to capital controls. It is claimed that floating rates have also allowed countries to choose trend inflation rates and to carry out effective anti-inflationary policies. These extra degrees of freedom would not be so prized in a world in which all countries consistently implemented sound and credible policies of their own accord. But, so the supporters of floating rates argue, they are valuable assets in the real world where one's trading partners can sometimes suffer quite serious lapses of discipline in macroeconomic policy.

Critics of the present system see the contribution of floating rates to monetary policy as more modest, if it exists at all. They note that whereas the exchange rate appreciation that goes with a tight monetary policy can aid the home country's anti-inflation efforts, it does so at the expense of handicapping the efforts of partner countries to control their own inflation rates; to them, it is thus a new type of "beggar-thy-neighbor" policy. They argue in addition that, at the margin, floating rates have not increased the independence of monetary policy all that much. After all, the considerable volume of official intervention during the floating rate period suggests that most industrial countries view the exchange rate as a policy target as well as a policy instrument.[50] When the exchange rate moves by a significant amount in a short period, even those countries whose exchange arrangements are classified as "independently floating" develop implicit exchange rate targets and adjust monetary policy accordingly. They also doubt whether floating rates have increased the potency of expansionary monetary policy. In this regard, they mention that: significant feedback effects of exchange rate depreciation on money, wages and prices limit the gain in competitiveness; J-curve effects in the response of the trade balance to exchange rate depreciation mean that, in the short to medium term, the external sector will weaken, not strengthen, the domestic impact of expansionary monetary policy; and that currency substitution can lead to much larger swings in exchange rates than the authorities may find desirable. Finally, the critics question whether mon-

etary policy ought to be geared toward domestic conditions. They contend that one of the main reasons why exchange rates have been so variable over the floating rate period is because monetary policy has not taken external considerations enough into account.[51]

## Resilience of Present System

Thus far, the appraisal of the present exchange rate system has been based on implicit comparisons with other exchange rate systems (including both those implemented in the past and those proposed for the future). Supporters of the present system question, however, whether, given the strains of the past decade (the major changes in the price of energy products, a number of important bank failures, sometimes large intercountry differences in inflation rates, monetary policies, and policy mixes, and so on), "any less flexible system would have survived" without increased reliance on restrictions on trade and capital flows.[52] The present system is thus viewed as being particularly resilient to the operating environment—no small advantage if it is assumed that there are significant costs associated with changing exchange rate systems.

To what is this resilience attributable? Three contributing factors might be identified.

First, the wide choice of exchange arrangements permitted by the Fund's Articles of Agreement means that it is possible to accommodate different country preference on the flexibility of exchange rates and the mix of domestic economic policies. Countries who feel that the benefits of fixed rates outweigh the costs can choose pegged exchange arrangements, while those that view exchange rate flexibility as essential can opt for floating. In between these two poles, there is room for adjustable pegs (the European Monetary System (EMS)) as well for different degrees of exchange market intervention within the group of countries classified as "independently floating." Supporters of the present system recall that the Bretton Woods system operated successfully while there was a consensus about the assignment of responsibilities for exchange rate action and monetary policy between the reserve-center country and others, but collapsed when this consensus evaporated. To the extent that the degree of exchange rate stability deemed appropriate differs from country to country, the present system can be said to be compatible with these differences.

---

[49] Group of Ten Report, paragraph 14.
[50] See Black (1980) and International Monetary Fund (1984c).

[51] "Exchange rate stability should be an important objective of policy instead of being a residual of other policy actions of individual countries, as is the case at present," Group of Twenty-Four Report, paragraph 65.
[52] Group of Ten Report, paragraph 14.

Second, the present system permits decentralized market-based decisions to act as a "safety valve" when it is not possible to reach centralized decisions about the sharing of the adjustment burden and about the equilibrium pattern of exchange rates. Because the market "takes a view," it is possible to avoid, so say the supporters of floating rates, the centralized management delays of the latter years of the Bretton Woods system.

Third, the present system contains enough "flex" in exchange rates to avoid what defenders of floating rates regard as the crucial flaw of all adjustable peg systems, namely, the incompatibility of high international mobility of capital and fixed exchange rates with narrow margins. They argue that so long as private market participants have greater resources than central banks, market views on exchange rates can change rapidly, and parities have to be changed from time to time to reflect changes in real economic conditions, any system that places tight limits on exchange rate movements will be subject to successful speculative attack; alternatively, attempts to preserve existing parities will force resort to increased restrictions on capital flows.

Critics of the present system acknowledge its resilience but argue that this is less important than its performance. They point out that the exchange rate system is basically a facilitating mechanism for more fundamental economic objectives, such as high employment, sustainable growth, price stability, and expanding and balanced international trade. Whatever its durability, an exchange rate system should be judged in terms of its contribution to those objectives. And on this scale, they find the present system of floating rates wanting.[53] They also maintain that the characteristics that make the present system relatively resilient may have other undesirable implications for its performance while it lasts. For example, the great diversity of exchange arrangements may make it more difficult to define "rules of the game" for macroeconomic policies that are sufficiently specific to be effective. Indeed, it is the very lack of such recognized rules of the game, especially for major industrial countries with floating rates that, according to critics, is responsible for the severe misalignments of the floating rate period. Similarly, while they agree that the present system allows the market "to take a view" when centralized decisions are not feasible, they argue that the present system does not offer a sufficient framework for reaching a satisfactory multilateral decision; in addition, the market's view is too often the "wrong" view. Finally, the same "flex" in exchange rates that provides a defense against "hot money" flows often proves a liability when exchange rates become divorced from fundamentals and get carried along by self-fulfilling destabilizing speculation.

## Proposals for Improving Exchange Rate Stability

As suggested earlier, both Reports conclude that the functioning of the exchange rate system needs to be improved. Both Reports also agree that perhaps the single most important element in achieving such an improvement lies in the better discipline and coordination of macroeconomic policies in the major industrial countries. The key question then is what mechanisms or channels, including Fund surveillance, are available for reaching that latter objective. Three types of proposals can be identified in the Group of Ten and Group of Twenty-Four Reports as ways of improving exchange rate stability: the adoption of "target zones" for the exchange rates of major currencies; the adoption of "objective indicators" or "targets" for macroeconomic policies in major industrial countries that could be used as a framework for the first stage of multilateral Fund surveillance; and the adoption of policy adjustments and of changes in the procedures for Fund surveillance that could be accomplished within existing exchange rate arrangements and the existing institutional framework for surveillance.

Since most of the specific reform proposals are for more automaticity in the adjustment and coordination process, it is perhaps useful as a prelude to describe how the present system stands on rules versus discretion in adjustment vis-à-vis alternative exchange rate systems.

If one were to classify alternative exchange rate systems along a spectrum according to either the degree of automaticity of the adjustment process, or the mix between rules and discretion in initiating adjustment, the present system would certainly stand closer to the complete discretion pole than the rules-only pole. In this respect, the pure gold standard with its (alleged) automatic specie-flow mechanism, the adjustable peg system with its clear implication for the subordination of domestic monetary policy to the exchange rate (except during fundamental disequilibrium), the objective indicator system with its automatic trigger for the initiation of adjustment discussions and actions, or even a pure floating system with its complete prohibition of all official intervention in the exchange market—all could be considered less discretionary than

---

[53] "The functioning of the present floating rate system has thus not been able to provide . . . a framework that facilitates the exchange of goods, services, and capital among countries, which sustains sound economic growth and helps develop orderly underlying conditions necessary for financial and economic stability," Group of Twenty-Four Report, paragraph 64.

the present system. By the same token, efforts at coordination of economic policies during the period of floating rates represent at most a middle ground between activist and passive coordination strategies. Efforts have gone beyond exchange of forecasts and policy intentions to encompass occasional common actions but have stopped well short of binding agreements on either exchange rate targets or the stance and mix of monetary and fiscal policies. The present system might therefore be characterized as "... a discretionary and decentralized system, with loose coordination among the main players but with tighter coordination and disaster relief during crises." [54] One way of characterizing the first two proposals for improving exchange rate stability—target zones and objective indicators—is to say that they seek to move the present system somewhat further in the direction of more automaticity and more centralization in adjustment and coordination. In contrast, the third proposal retains the discretionary, decentralized character of the present system but counts on "enhanced dialogue and persuasion through peer pressure" to make the available channels for adjustment and coordination function better than they have in the past.

## Target Zones for Exchange Rates of Major Currencies

One proposal for improving exchange rate stability that is specifically addressed in both the Reports is the adoption of target zones for the exchange rates of major currencies. As indicated earlier, the Group of Twenty-Four Deputies felt that the adoption of target zones "could help achieve the objective of exchange rate stability and a sustainable pattern of payments balances." [55] In contrast, the majority of Group of Ten Deputies considered that "... the adoption of target zones is undesirable and in any case impractical in current circumstances."[56]

In this subsection, attention is focused on three questions: what is meant by a target-zone approach to exchange rate management; what is the rationale for it; and what is behind the skepticism about and/or the opposition to, that proposal.

In the Group of Ten Report, target zones are described as follows: "... the authorities concerned would define wide margins around an adjustable set of exchange rates devised to be consistent with a sustainable pattern of balances of payments." [57]

Target zones differ from the present system of floating rates in two respects: the authorities establish a target zone for the exchange rate for some future period; and the authorities partially direct monetary policy to the exchange rate to discourage the exchange rate from moving outside its zone. Target zones differ from "pure" or "clean" floating in that the authorities are permitted to intervene in the exchange market, and indeed, are encouraged "to take a view" on the desirable level of the exchange rate. At the same time, there are no formal or rigid commitments to intervene in exchange markets in all circumstances—a characteristic that differentiates target zones from the adjustable peg system. Finally, in addition to the absence of a formal intervention obligation, target zones differ from a system of rigidly fixed rates in that the zones themselves are to be occasionally reviewed and changed if deemed necessary (to reflect, for example, differential inflation and any need for balance of payments adjustment).

Most target zone proposals envisage the members as being the five largest industrial countries. Other countries could then "fix" or "flex" on the members of the target zones as they saw fit. Target zones would reflect estimates of real equilibrium exchange rates because the real exchange rate is the most relevant rate for resource allocation and balance of payments adjustment; however, for operational purposes, they would be defined in terms of nominal exchange rates. Monetary policy and exchange market intervention are viewed as the two policy instruments to be used for external balance while monetary and fiscal policy are assumed to be adequate to the task of countering "inflationary and deflationary pressures." [58]

It is possible to conceive of a whole spectrum of possible approaches to target zones. The various approaches could be distinguished by reference to the following four characteristics: the width of the target zones (outside of which the exchange rate is viewed as "out of line"); the frequency of changes in the target zones; the degree of publicity given to the zones (such as public announcement versus confidential disclosure in official circles, or "loud zones" versus "quiet zones"); and the degree of commitment to keeping exchange rates within the zone.

At one end of the spectrum, "hard" target zones would imply narrow margins, infrequently revised zones, public announcement of the zones, and a monetary policy that was directed at keeping the exchange rate within the zone. In this sense, hard

---

[54] International Monetary Fund (1984c).
[55] Group of Twenty-Four Report, paragraph 66.
[56] Group of Ten Report, paragraph 32. A more thorough treatment of the target zone proposal, particularly of its technical and operational aspects, can be found in Frenkel and Goldstein (1986).

[57] Group of Ten Report, paragraph 31.
[58] Group of Twenty-Four Report, paragraph 67.

target zones might be considered a close relative of the EMS' fixed but adjustable parities with narrow margins and a "divergence indicator." Unlike the EMS, however, there would be no rigid commitment to exchange rate intervention; nor do hard target zones imply any analogue to the credit facilities of the EMS.

At the other end of the spectrum, "soft" target zones would be characterized by wide, frequently-revised, confidential zones, and by a monetary policy that pays only limited attention to the level of the exchange rate. Soft target zones differ from existing procedures for Fund surveillance (such as, the requirement for reporting real exchange rate changes in excess of 10 percent to the Executive Board) in that the former introduces a more explicit and formal framework for defining the appropriate pattern of exchange rates and for specifying the links between exchange rates and macroeconomic policies.[59]

## Rationale for Target Zones

Supporters of target zones make essentially six arguments about why and how target zones will improve the functioning of the exchange rate system.

First, target zones are said to improve the international consistency (that is, coordination) of macroeconomic policies because target zones have to be negotiated and must display mutual consistency of cross exchange rates.[60] In this way, so it is argued, the exchange rate implications of alternative stances and mixes of macroeconomic policies will be directly confronted, thereby ending the undesirable current practice whereby exchange rates emerge as a residual of other policy actions of individual countries.[61] In a related vein, supporters argue that the negotiation and revision of target zones could act as a convenient organizing framework for multilateral surveillance. Even if the zones were wide and frequently revised, they would catch the most flagrant and persistent cases of inappropriate policies. Thus, while soft zones might not be able to identify real exchange rate misalignments of 10 percent or less, they would, so it is claimed, at least prevent the 30 percent or larger misalignments that do so much damage to the system.

Second, target zones may improve the discipline of macroeconomic policies in two ways: if exchange rates are maintained within the zones, then monetary and fiscal policy will be disciplined by the exchange rate constraint, much as in a fixed rate system; and if the authorities opt to alter the zone rather than their policies, they will still have to explain why a new zone is appropriate and convince other members accordingly. The latter requirement could be said to introduce stronger peer pressure into policy formulation.

Third, target zones are viewed as providing an anchor for medium-term exchange rate expectations, thereby promoting stabilizing speculation and greater stability of exchange rates.[62] The anchor is said to be established on two counts: the obligation (albeit an informal one) or the intention to keep the exchange rate within the zone gives market participants valuable information about the future course of monetary policy, thereby lessening the danger that short-term deviations of policy will be erroneously extrapolated into the future; and the publication of target zones gives the market a direct estimate of the equilibrium exchange rate (plus or minus the width of the zone), thereby lessening the risk that the "wrong" model is used to link policies and exchange rates. Target zones can thus also be seen as ensuring that "convergence of economic performance" is "sufficient" rather than just "necessary" for lasting exchange rate stability.[63]

Fourth, because the likely members of a target zone system would be the key-currency industrial countries, it is claimed that target zones would reduce the asymmetry in adjustment that has plagued the present exchange rate system. In particular, it would subject the countries whose policies have the greatest spillover effects on the world economy to the same scrutiny and pressure experienced by smaller countries with external and internal imbalances. And the perception that Fund surveillance was evenhanded would, so it is argued, make it more effective on the smaller countries as well.

Fifth, while proponents recognize that there are difficulties associated with identifying equilibrium exchange rates, they point out that "arriving at a judgment about the appropriateness of the exchange rate of a currency is part of the current practices of the IMF."[64] As such, these difficulties should not be exaggerated.

Finally, while it is acknowledged that many of the factors associated with the collapse of the Bretton

---

[59] Existing procedures do not rely on the assessment of appropriate zones but rather use as a starting point the last occasion on which exchange rate developments were brought to the attention of the Executive Board. In addition, this reporting and monitoring procedure has not led to any Board discussions.

[60] "... commitment to [target zones for exchange rates of major countries]... would promote greater international policy consistency," Group of Twenty-Four Report, paragraph 66.

[61] "They [target zones] could ... trigger consultations that would induce step by step, more direct links between domestic policies and exchange rate considerations," Group of Ten Report, paragraph 31.

[62] "They [some Deputies] further believe that credible commitments to target zones would contribute to stabilizing market expectations...," Group of Ten Report, paragraph 31.

[63] Group of Ten Report, paragraph 31.

[64] Group of Ten Report, paragraph 31.

Woods system have not gone away, supporters maintain that target zones can survive speculative attacks. They reason that so long as target zones are revised frequently to reflect inflation differentials and the need for real exchange rate adjustment, the large and discrete changes in exchange rates that motivate speculative attacks will not occur. Also, they point to the durability and success of the EMS as tangible proof that an adjustable peg system can survive in the 1980s; since target zones share some of the EMS' characteristics, the former too can be considered practical.

## Opposition to Target Zones

Concerns about the desirability and practicality of target zones can be summarized in the following arguments.

• There are doubts about the extent to which target zones will promote coordination and discipline in macroeconomic policy among the members. It can be argued that by focusing attention on exchange rates rather than on the root cause of misalignment—namely, the stance, mix, and divergence of policies—one may lessen the pressures for corrective action. Also, some would say that evidence from periods during which exchange rates were more rigid does not suggest that there was more complete, faster, or more symmetrical external adjustment. So why then should target zones induce better discipline and coordination when regimes with more formal commitments did not? Further, reaching a consensus on the zones of desirable exchange rates could prove difficult.[65] This raises two additional dangers: the process of negotiating target zones could produce serious frictions among the members, possibly reducing future coordination in this and other areas; lack of consensus could reproduce the centralized-management delays of the latter years of the Bretton Woods system, with serious misalignments then stemming from too little nominal exchange rate flexibility.

• The claim that target zones would provide an anchor for exchange rate expectations can be challenged. Opponents of target zones argue that because our knowledge about the determinants of exchange rate changes is so imperfect, zones would have to be wide enough to reflect that ignorance. Also, the zones will need to be revised to reflect changes in real economic conditions. But then wide, moving zones will not, so its opponents claim, provide a useful anchor for exchange rate expectations.[66] What is more, some would add that if the lack of an anchor under the present system reflects uncertainty about future policies, the way to overcome that problem is to announce the future course of policies, not of exchange rates.

• A third criticism about these target zones is that they do not resolve the problem of how to allocate the burden of adjustment among member countries. When more than one country's (effective) exchange rate leaves the zone, it will be necessary to specify who does what. The target zone proposal does not, so it is argued, solve the "n-1 problem."

• Skeptics of target zones also reason that since markets would inevitably test them, they could only be defended if monetary policy was diverted rather markedly from its domestic stabilization duties to stabilizing the exchange rate. But this raises the question of which policy instruments would then be in charge of maintaining internal balance (that is, price stability and sustainable growth). The answer might be fiscal policy, but some would say that experience raises serious doubts about whether it would be adequate to, and flexible enough for, that task. In such a case, the constraints imposed on monetary policy by a target zone might, in the view of opponents, handicap efforts to achieve stable prices and high employment over the medium-term.[67]

• Another concern is that the exchange rate may send false signals about both the need for adjustment and the appropriate corrective action. This is another way of asking whether the exchange rate would be a "sufficient statistic" for guiding macroeconomic policies. Some observers answer that question in the negative. The Group of Ten Report, for example, concludes that while exchange rate developments ". . . provide information on private markets' assessments of underlying economic conditions and of current and expected policies, . . . a wide range of factors beyond exchange rate developments should also be taken into account in assessing national policies and the need for consultation and policy discussion."[68]

An example may illustrate the potential pitfalls involved. Suppose an overvalued real exchange rate primarily reflected a structural budget deficit in the home country. Then a (simplistic) application of the target-zone approach would point toward the need for

---

[65] "Most Deputies, however, are of the view that reaching a consensus on the range of desirable exchange rates [for target zones] would prove extremely difficult," Group of Ten Report, paragraph 32.

[66] "Given our imperfect knowledge of the determinants of exchange rate movements, the target zones would have to be too wide to serve as an anchor for expectations," Group of Ten Report, paragraph 32.

[67] "Above all, the constraints imposed on domestic policies by target zones might undermine efforts to pursue sound and stable policies in a medium-term framework," Group of Ten Report, paragraph 32.

[68] Group of Ten Report, paragraph 30.

monetary expansion (in the home country) to depreciate the actual exchange rate—and this even though the root cause of the problem lay with fiscal policy.[69] More generally, target zone systems that rely on monetary policy to keep rates within zones can be criticized as being ill suited to handling disequilibria that derive from inappropriate policy mixes. In short, critics argue that target zones are not a sufficient statistic because money supply changes are not the appropriate response to all types of disturbances. This danger would be reduced if target zones were seen solely as a trigger mechanism for multilateral discussion of policies, with the appropriate policy response determined on a case-by-case basis. But then, opponents of target zones argue, the system will lose its "automatic" character and may not increase the speed of adjustment at all.

• Last but not least, opponents of target zones warn that the experience of the EMS cannot necessarily be generalized to a "broader and more heterogeneous context characterized by the presence of a plurality of reserve currencies."[70] To them, the policy convergence and exchange rate stability associated with the EMS cannot be divorced from the unusual degree of political commitment behind it, the capital controls retained by some members, and the structural characteristics of the member countries.[71]

## Objective Indicators

A second specific proposal for improving exchange rate stability and for strengthening the analytical basis of Fund surveillance, is to introduce a set of "objective indicators" or "targets" for macroeconomic outcomes and policies into the multilateral discussion and negotiation of macroeconomic policies in key-currency countries. This proposal is presented in paragraph 78 of the Group of Twenty-Four Report as follows:

> "Multilateral surveillance and bilateral (Article IV) consultations should form two stages of the surveillance process, rather than two parallel operations. The first stage would involve multilateral discussions and negotiations to be conducted on a regular basis within the framework of the IMF about a mutually consistent set of objectives, and a set of policies to collectively achieve these objectives. The aim might be to search for a set of outcomes or 'objective indicators' or 'targets,' that appear to be sustainable in the medium term and desirable to all parties. This should be quite feasible when the multilateral surveillance exercise is limited to a few major industrial countries, such as the key currency countries. The second stage would involve a comparison between the actual outcomes and the recommended targets or indicators, and a discussion of what measures would be appropriate when the two differ. This stage might most efficiently be conducted on a bilateral basis as part of Article IV consultations."

Although the Group of Twenty-Four Report is not explicit about what form domestic policy-oriented targets would take, it might be assumed that they would cover the major targets of policy (such as rates of inflation and unemployment, the growth of real output, the balance of payments, fiscal positions, and possibly, the exchange rate), as well as some of the major policy instruments (the money supply, government expenditures, taxes, or structural measures); presumably, they would be framed in a medium-term setting.

In principle, the process of setting targets and instruments should be similar to that which explicitly or implicitly takes place in national governments, with of course the important distinction that the process would be multilateral. The targets could be specific numbers, or ranges or zones, or if even more flexibility was required, simply obligations to avoid large or sudden changes in the chosen variable. Perhaps the best analogy in a domestic context is the setting of official targets for the growth rates of monetary aggregates. Such targets provide a presumption that the authorities will conduct policies so that the growth rates of aggregates would evolve within the specified ranges. If the targeted aggregate moves outside its expected range, it is presumed that the authorities will act to counter this movement, or will explain why the earlier target is no longer appropriate. Even when the targets are not always attained, they provide, so their supporters argue, a relatively straightforward way of monitoring and explaining the authorities actions; also, when the targets are announced, they may provide an anchor for expectations.

### Rationale Behind Objective Indicators or Targets

The case for objective indicators or targets for macroeconomic policies can be said to have five elements.

First, such indicators or targets address directly the perceived main cause of exchange rate misalignment,

---

[69] Supporters of target zones deny that an intelligent application of target zones would produce such perverse policy prescriptions. In their view, the political pressures that would emanate from repeated breaches of the zones would yield the appropriate corrective policies, both as regards the stance and mix of policies.

[70] Group of Ten Report, paragraph 24.

[71] Proponents of target zones might reply that successful policy coordination, whatever the exchange rate regime, requires precisely such "unusual" political commitment.

namely, the lack of soundness and international consistency in the macroeconomic policies of the major industrial countries. In contrast with target zones, policy targets or objective indicators bypass what some may regard as the uncertain link between exchange rate movements and the stance of monetary and fiscal policies. Here, the desired target values or ranges for all major policy instruments can be specified directly and their implications for exchange rates can be estimated. As such, vague policy intentions, such as "keeping more of an eye" on the exchange rate in the conduct of domestic monetary policy, are replaced with specific and verifiable policy commitments, for example, that the money supplies in countries A and B will be targeted to grow by x and y percent, respectively, over the next six months.

Second, the indicator or target proposal can be used as a "trigger mechanism" to activate coordinated discussions of how recognized departures of actual from desired macroeconomic outcomes can best be remedied. For example, the Group of Twenty-Four proposal envisages such discussion on a bilateral basis as part of the Fund's Article IV consultations whenever actual outcomes differ from recommended targets or indicators. In this way, the perceived lethargy in adjustment under the present discretion-based system may be overcome. The use of objective indicators to improve the speed of adjustment is of course well known from the work of the Committee of Twenty.[72]

A third advantage of the target-indicator proposal is said to be that it pays attention to the level of, as well as to the inter-country differences in, macroeconomic policies. To some observers, this gives it an edge over proposals that use the exchange rate to signal a misalignment of policies. For example, if two countries both inflate at 10 percent, their bilateral exchange rate may be stable but few would agree that their macroeconomic policy stances were right. By focusing on the appropriate setting of policy targets and instruments within as well as across countries, the target-indicator proposal is said to overcome this danger.

Fourth, because the target-indicator proposal is likely to encompass a broad set of policy targets and policy instruments, it could be argued that it is less susceptible than is say, a target zone scheme, to sending "wrong signals" about either the need for adjustment or the proper policy remedy for adjustment. Thus, one can monitor directly not only the exchange rate but also such variables as growth, inflation, employment, or the pattern of payments balances; similarly, departures of actual from targeted outcomes might be met not merely by altering monetary policy but by other mixes of policies (including structural measures) if deemed appropriate.

Finally, supporters of this proposal might argue that, despite some potential difficulties in negotiating and interpreting the targets and indicators, it is operational. As supporting evidence, they could cite the use of quantitative indicators and targets in domestic monetary policy in many industrial countries. In addition, they might note that the target-indicator proposal is a close relative of the program targets and quantitative "performance criteria" employed by the Fund in its stabilization programs. It might be argued that if these objective indicators and targets have been used to good effect by the Fund for over 35 years in the formulation of stabilization programs for a diverse set of countries, why cannot a similar approach be followed in designing coordinated "shadow programs" for key-currency industrial countries, especially when the systemic consequences of inappropriate domestic policies are so much greater for the latter group of countries? In addition, such an approach would, so its supporters argue, constitute an effective remedy for the current "asymmetry" in the exercise of Fund surveillance.

## Opposition to Objective Indicators or Targets

Both the advisability and practicality of objective indicators or targets for coordinated macroeconomic policy formulation remain controversial. At least five counter-arguments might be offered in opposition to this proposal.

To begin with, it might be argued that it would be even harder to reach a consensus on a range of desirable policy targets and policy instruments than it would on a range of desirable exchange rates.[73] There would simply be too many parameters on which to obtain agreement. And the more specific the desired policy commitments, the more difficult would be the negotiations. Some would say that it is one thing to argue that major industrial countries should "take account" of external repercussions in setting domestic policies, but quite another to argue that they should be dominated by external considerations. Also, if policy responses to target departures have to be multilaterally negotiated and agreed, then the administrative problems become, according to the critics, even more

---

[72] See particularly "The Report of the Technical Group on Indicators," International Monetary Fund (1974).

[73] Kenen (1985, p.11), for example, in weighing options for reforming the international monetary system concludes: "... it should be much easier, technically and politically, for governments to collaborate in managing exchange rates than to coordinate their monetary and fiscal policies in a timely manner."

burdensome. Indeed, some would conclude that if a set of instruments and targets had to be multilaterally negotiated, the constraints on national sovereignty would be even more severe than in a rigid fixed rate system; hence, such a proposal is unlikely to be acceptable to most members.

A second criticism of the target-indicator proposal is that if it simply triggers discussions on the appropriate coordination of macroeconomic policies, it will not allocate and enforce adjustment among the countries involved. Thus, unlike say, the gold standard, the target-indicator proposal does not offer any "rules" on how to eliminate recognized disequilibria.

Third, although use of a broad set of indicators and targets may send fewer false signals about the need for adjustment than reliance on a single indicator (such as the exchange rate), opponents argue that it will still send more false signals than a judgmental appraisal that goes beyond such indicators. With any mechanistic formula, there is always the danger that events and factors unforeseen at the time that policy targets are set will intrude and cause deviations between actual outcomes and targets; hence, the indicators would have to be reviewed judgmentally in any case. As evidence of the importance of such "news," opponents note that past forecasting errors for such outcome variables as current accounts and exchange rates have been very large indeed.[74] Further, when many indicators are used, they may point in different directions.

Fourth, just as it is difficult to agree on an operational definition of the equilibrium exchange rate, it may also be difficult to agree on internationally consistent, quantifiable indicators of monetary and fiscal policies (to say nothing of structural policies). Which monetary aggregate should be used as the indicator? Should the fiscal deficit or surplus be measured at the central or general government level, and should it be adjusted for cyclical factors?

Finally, opponents of the target-indicator proposal might doubt whether the use of quantitative indicators in a national setting carries any implications for their feasibility in a multilateral setting. They could argue that at the national level authorities can be confident that if quantitative policy targets prove less helpful than anticipated, their use can be modified or even discarded. In this connection, several major industrial countries have, in fact, ceased establishing monetary targets or indicated that they would place less reliance on them in the future. No such flexibility could be assured for any single member country in a multilateral setting. In addition, they might point to the often lengthy negotiations of quantitative policy targets in Fund programs. It might also be argued that industrial countries would not face the same external financing constraint as program countries and, therefore, would be under less pressure to reach agreement on indicators. What is the outlook then for negotiating a mutually agreeable set of these targets among five major industrial countries, and what would happen in the meantime if such discussions broke down? In short, opponents might argue that what is feasible with quantitative policy targets on a national level may not be so in a multilateral setting.

## Improvements Within Existing Institutional Setting

As noted earlier, the Group of Ten Report concludes that "... the fundamental approach of the Articles [of Agreement of the Fund] remains valid and ... the key elements of the current ... system require no major institutional change,"[75] and that "... no major changes are required in the present institutional setting for exercising surveillance over national policies."[76] Instead, the Group of Ten Report recommends that improvements be sought within the framework of the present system. These improvements would focus on the following four areas.

First, "... the adoption of sound, credible, and stable policies"[77] at the national level, especially in major countries, would contribute "fundamentally" to exchange rate stability. Also, the "... liberalization of capital markets and, more broadly, removal of restrictions and structural rigidities"[78] so as to reduce the burden placed on foreign exchange markets in absorbing short-term disturbances would, so it is argued, reduce the short-run volatility of exchange rates.

Second, "... in setting national policies, the international implications and interactions of those policies should receive an appropriately high priority."[79] This, it is argued, would improve the compatibility of policies among countries and the convergence of economic performance around sustainable non-inflationary growth. As such, it would lead to greater exchange market stability. To achieve better international coordination of policies, "... close and continuing cooperation among countries and a strengthening of international surveillance"[80] are identified as central elements.

---

[74] See Willett (1977) and Mussa (1983).

[75] Group of Ten Report, paragraph 97.
[76] Group of Ten Report, paragraph 36.
[77] Group of Ten Report, paragraph 28.
[78] Group of Ten Report, paragraph 28.
[79] Group of Ten Report, paragraph 29.
[80] Group of Ten Report, paragraph 33.

Third, strengthened surveillance should be built on "... enhanced dialogue and persuasion through peer pressure rather than mechanically imposed external constraints."[81] Specific measures to strengthen surveillance cover both bilateral and multilateral surveillance.

Among the proposals for improving bilateral surveillance that appear in the Group of Ten Report are those that address the policymaking level at which governments are represented in the consultation process; the possibility of a confidential exchange of views between the Managing Director and the Finance Minister at the end of the consultation process for important countries; the degree of candor in the assessment of national policies and of their international impact; identification of necessary improvements in the scope, quality, and timeliness of data; improvements in analytical techniques; the use of supplemental surveillance techniques; and the continued development of enhanced surveillance procedures. In addition, mention was made of the publicity to be given to the outcome of the consultation process and to other Fund reports and summings-up.

Turning to multilateral surveillance, the Group of Ten Report proposes that there be "... a separate chapter" of the *World Economic Outlook* devoted to "... analyzing the repercussions of national policies of Group of Ten countries and of their interaction in the determination of exchange rate developments and international adjustment."[82] In addition, the Group of Ten Report proposes that the Group of Ten should review the conclusions of this chapter, when appropriate, at Ministerial level.

Finally, the Group of Ten Report argues that "... neither capital controls nor intervention can be relied upon to attain lasting stability of exchange rates."[83] On official intervention, the Group of Ten Report endorses the conclusions reached in the Report of the Working Group on Exchange Market Intervention (1983). With respect to controls on international capital flows, this Report concludes that such controls would carry "substantial" economic costs and that free capital movements are beneficial to "... the expansion of trade and to efficient resource allocation."[84]

## Rationale for Seeking Improvements Within Present Institutional Setting

Although the Group of Ten conclusion for seeking improvements in exchange rate stability within present institutional arrangements encompasses a wide and diverse set of proposals, it is possible to describe (as was done with the two proposals analyzed earlier) the underlying rationale. This rationale might be said to rest on the following five arguments.

First, supporters argue that the observed weaknesses in the functioning of the present system of floating rates reflect not design flaws in the exchange rate system per se but rather flaws of implementation in the underlying macroeconomic and structural policies. Until national governments themselves muster the requisite political will to adopt sound, credible, and stable policies, no exchange rate system—be it one of very low or very high flexibility of nominal exchange rates—will work properly. Conversely, when national governments do so act, proposals for altering the nature of exchange arrangements would not be necessary. Supporters therefore argue that energy ought to be concentrated on ways of bringing this improved policy implementation into being. "Enhanced dialogue" and "peer pressure" represent in their view the most hopeful routes to that end. The existing channels of surveillance could be used more effectively and coordinated better to support these efforts.

Second, after over a decade of experience with floating rates, it is clear that it is neither realistic nor helpful to believe that each country can decide independently its own policy stance and mix and allow the exchange rate to settle all conflicts in the market place. It is not realistic because floating rates are not capable in any case of providing enough insulation to make independent targeting work. It is not helpful because failure to take other countries policies and objectives into account will only induce in the long run retaliatory actions which, in turn, will make the path to internal and external balance slower and less satisfactory than if some coordination of policies was carried out. Improved coordination of policies would do much to reduce the large swings in real exchange rates that have characterized the last thirteen years. Again, supporters of the existing framework argue that the way to get such better coordination is through close and continuing cooperation not via "mechanically-imposed external constraints."

Third, no exchange rate system can provide full insulation from the effects of policies and disturbances abroad. Nevertheless, exchange rate volatility and overshooting could be much reduced if restrictions and structural rigidities in goods, labor, and capital markets were dismantled. In this way, asset prices, particularly exchange rates, would not have to compensate so much for the stickiness of wages and prices. Exchange rates would still of course show variability but, so it is argued, this variability would not necessarily be "excessive."

---

[81] Group of Ten Report, paragraph 38.
[82] Group of Ten Report, paragraph 51.
[83] Group of Ten Report, paragraph 27.
[84] Group of Ten Report, paragraph 25.

Fourth, exchange rate developments can provide some useful information on the market's appraisal of macroeconomic policies. In some cases, the market's appraisal may not be consistent with fundamentals and authorities will want to make known their own views (as they did through the September 1985 Group of Five Agreement in New York). This however, will be more the exception than the rule. Similarly, (pre-announced) quantitative targets for macroeconomic policies, especially monetary policy, may be useful in certain circumstances in providing an anchor for expectations. But, so the argument goes, neither exchange rates nor quantitative targets can substitute for judgmental assessments about the appropriate course of policies over the medium term. To replace the latter with the former would endanger the achievement of price stability and sustainable growth. Also, experience suggests to defenders of the existing framework that automatic adjustment rules usually turn out to be less automatic in practice than in theory, and that very specific adjustment or policy rules can become liabilities when the global environment changes in unexpected ways.

Fifth, those supporting improvements within the existing system find no presumption that the resource allocation costs from impeding the international flow of capital would be any less serious than those associated with restrictions on trade flows. Also, they note that even aggressive capital control programs (such as those of the early 1970s) often failed to stem private capital flows, and the subsequent development of offshore banking could be seen as making their efficacy today even less likely. As regards official intervention, they could point to a large body of empirical evidence that strongly suggests that non-sterilized intervention is unlikely to have a lasting impact on the level of the exchange rate.[85] Nevertheless, intervention can in their view be useful in: countering disorderly market conditions; reducing short-term volatility; complementing and supporting other policies; and expressing an attitude toward exchange markets.

## Opposition to Operating Within Existing Institutional Setting

The arguments in favor of improving exchange rate stability via the existing institutional setting have not gone unchallenged. The case against that position might be said to rest on the following arguments.

First, while acknowledging the fundamental role played by sound, credible, and stable policies in achieving a stable system of exchange rates under all types of exchange arrangements, it could be argued that a good exchange rate system must offer the right incentives and pressures for responsible policy conduct. On the basis of experience with floating rates, it might be concluded that floating rates have been wanting on that score; they have not promoted the right policies. Further, while "enhanced dialogue and peer pressure" may be necessary elements for improving policy behavior, they are unlikely under this view to be sufficient. In short, some would say that the choice is not policy reform or exchange rate reform but rather how best to design the exchange rate system to achieve policy reform. For this reason, the "incentive," "pressure," and "trigger" features of target zones, or at least of some concerted "views" on exchange rates (as seem to be developing since September 22, 1985), should—so the argument goes—not be dismissed.

Second, while it could easily be accepted that better coordination of policies would reduce the large and persistent misalignments of real exchange rates observed in the past, and that such coordination requires "close and continuing cooperation," it might again be maintained that some external constraint is essential to obtain that cooperation.[86] Modes of coordination that do not send clear, regular, and strong signals about when, what, and how to coordinate can be viewed as ineffective. This in turn leads opponents of the existing framework to the conclusion that substantive strengthening of both the principles and procedures of Fund surveillance is probably necessary.

Third, it might be conceded that target zones (or concerted views on exchange rates) and objective indicators would occasionally lead to the wrong diagnosis and the wrong remedy for external adjustment. Nevertheless, these adjustment mechanisms might still be regarded as performing better on average than a judgmental mechanism that sometimes doesn't initiate adjustment at all, and sometimes, by its inaction, encourages other more costly forms of adjustment (such as protectionism). It might also be argued that the constraints placed on domestic monetary policy in the EMS have not unduly handicapped efforts to achieve price stability and sustainable growth. Furthermore, critics of the existing framework might argue that while the recent Group of Five initiative was welcome, it would have been even more welcome if it had taken place in 1982 or 1983 and if authorities had on a more regular basis spoken out against market-

---

[85] Report of the Working Group on Exchange Market Intervention (1983), Rogoff (1984), Obstfeld (1985).

[86] "In the meantime, a mechanism has to be devised to enforce policy coordination among the major industrial countries," Group of Twenty-Four Report, paragraph 5.

determined misalignments of key-currency exchange rates.

Fourth, while liberalization of capital and trade flows might be regarded as an effective means of dampening exchange rate overshooting in countries with "... diversified economies and high mobility of factors of production,"[87] its applicability to developing countries might be questioned. Here, the arguments (as presented in the Group of Twenty-Four Report) are that protection of infant industries, judiciously applied, may be indispensable to diversification and development, and that controls to limit capital flows may become "... necessary for the stability of exchange and interest rates."[88]

Finally, some have argued that even in industrial countries, impediments to capital flows (such as round-tripping taxes) need to be seriously evaluated.[89] It is not that such impediments would be costless. They would not. But these costs are viewed by supporters of such proposals as smaller than the macroeconomic costs associated with larger exchange rate fluctuations under free mobility of capital. Under this view, the answer to excessive volatility of exchange rates is to "throw some sand" into the wheels of the efficient world capital market, not to apply more grease to those wheels. On intervention, a case might be made that the potential for increasing its effectiveness by combining it with other policy measures has not yet been fully realized. As an example, it might be argued that developments since the Group of Five agreement in September 1985 are consistent with the position that official views on deviations of exchange rates from fundamentals, in combination with intervention and with some prospects of an improvement in fundamentals, can be effective in "pricking" a speculative bubble in the exchange markets.

---

[87] Group of Twenty-Four Report, paragraph 70.
[88] Group of Twenty-Four Report, paragraph 87.
[89] Tobin (1980).

# II  Surveillance Over Exchange Rate Policies

The Articles of Agreement of the International Monetary Fund, as amended in 1978, provide that member countries can adopt exchange arrangements of their choice, other than a peg to gold. The amended articles also specify certain general obligations of members and require the Fund to "exercise firm surveillance over the exchange rate policies of members and [to] adopt specific principles for the guidance of all members with respect to those policies" (Article IV, Section 3(b)). In preparation for the entry into force of the amended Articles, the Executive Board adopted in 1977 the document "Surveillance over Exchange Policies" (see Appendix III).[90]

This chapter assesses experience with the principles of surveillance over the period that they have been in operation. The decision adopting the surveillance document provides for its review every two years, so that there have already been a number of assessments of the surveillance principles. These have resulted in a number of modifications in the way in which the Fund's surveillance activities are conducted. However, the basic document has not been amended.

The fact that the surveillance document has not been changed does not, it should be emphasized, reflect a feeling of satisfaction with the way in which surveillance has operated. In fact, past reviews have revealed widespread concern that the objectives of Fund surveillance are not being fully met. However, it has generally been felt that the source of the problem lay more with the policies pursued by individual countries than with the language of the surveillance document. This language was regarded as sufficiently broad to permit the Fund to express views on the whole range of policies affecting international economic developments. It was feared that attempting to make it more specific would meet with disagreement and might not be in accordance with the requirement of the Articles of Agreement that . . . "these [surveillance] principles shall respect the domestic social and political policies of members, and in applying these principles, the Fund shall pay due regard to the circumstances of members" (Article IV, Section 3(b)).[91]

For several reasons, however, it seemed appropriate that the 1986 review should involve a more thoroughgoing reappraisal of the basic principles of surveillance. In the first place, concerns about exchange rate variability had, if anything, intensified in the preceding years, as noted in chapter I of this study. Exchange rate variability had become a more troubling feature of international economic relationships than was expected at the time the decision was adopted. This applied both to short-run exchange rate volatility and, more particularly, to longer-term exchange rate swings. Second, it had become increasingly clear that the management of the debt difficulties facing developing countries could be hampered by inappropriate policies affecting exchange rates and by unpredictable exchange market developments. This conclusion applied both to the exchange rate policies of heavily indebted countries themselves, and to exchange rate developments among their industrial country trading partners. These latter developments can have major implications for the real cost of servicing debt, as well as for the strength of protectionist sentiment.

A third reason for reconsidering the surveillance document was the attention given to the functioning of the exchange rate system and the subject of surveillance in the Reports of the Group of Ten and the Group of Twenty-Four released in 1985. Both of these reports devoted considerable attention to the subject of surveillance, and made recommendations for improvements. The Group of Ten Report notes that surveillance had not been as effective as desirable in bringing about needed policy changes. The appropriate response to these shortcomings was felt by the Group of Ten Deputies to lie in a strengthening of existing mechanisms for encouraging better policies rather than in major changes in the institutional structure for surveillance itself. Nevertheless, the report invited the

---

[90] The Executive Board Decision adopting the document (No. 5392-77/63) was taken on April 29, 1977 and took effect when the Second Amendment to the Articles entered into force on April 1, 1978. See *Selected Decisions of the International Monetary Fund and Selected Documents* (Washington: IMF, twelfth issue, 1986), p. 10. The document is given in full in Appendix III.

[91] It is also provided that there should be annual reviews of the manner in which the surveillance decision is implemented.

Fund's Executive Board to review the surveillance decision with a view to facilitating greater use of supplementary surveillance procedures, and made a number of other suggestions that could involve changes in the text of the surveillance document. In addition, some Deputies from the Group of Ten countries expressed interest in exploring the technical aspects of target zone proposals.

The Report of the Group of Twenty-Four went further than that of the Group of Ten in suggesting changes in the existing mechanisms of surveillance, and contained several proposals that would require changes in the language of the surveillance document. The report stated, inter alia, that "Surveillance . . . should be explicitly recognized as surveillance of the international adjustment process." It proposed the use of "target zones" for exchange rates as a means for achieving greater exchange rate stability, and put forward the concept of exchange rate misalignment as a criterion or trigger for multilateral consultations. All these proposals would require changes in the surveillance decision to give them effect.

The next section of this chapter sets out the background to the surveillance decision, indicating the prevailing view of international economic interactions at the time that decision was adopted, and the perceived scope and limitations of the surveillance mechanism. (As part of this background, this section also covers earlier experience with the "Guidelines for Floating" which were adopted in 1974 and effectively lapsed with the 1977 decision.) The chapter then considers developments in the nine years or so following the adoption of the surveillance document. The purpose of this is to identify those aspects of the world economy that differed from the evolution that was foreseen in 1977, and to consider the implications of these differences for the content and role of exchange rate surveillance. The final section of the chapter considers ways in which the existing surveillance document might be changed in the light of the preceding analysis. This section also considers those procedural suggestions that would involve changing the language of the 1977 decision. Appendix III reproduces the 1977 decision, and the supplemental procedure introduced in 1979.

## Guidelines for Floating, 1974

During the period of the par value system, the Fund had frequently expressed views on members' economic policies in general, and on the effectiveness of their adjustment policies in particular. A body of experience had been accumulated concerning how to define what constituted a "fundamental disequilibrium" that would justify exchange rate action. However, little attention had been devoted to developing a code for economic policymaking that would be applicable in circumstances where most major currencies were floating. The need for such a code became apparent during 1973–74, when it grew clear that flexible rates among major currencies would probably endure for a considerable period.

The "Guidelines for the Management of Floating Exchange Rates" were adopted on June 13, 1974.[92] They were based on an analytical view of the world in which:

(1) it was considered possible to make an operationally meaningful distinction between policies being used for balance of payments purposes, and policies used for other purposes;

(2) balance of payments equilibrium could be defined as a situation in which the current account surplus or deficit was equal to "normal" capital flows plus reserve accumulation;

(3) "normal" capital flows could be identified on the basis of slow-moving historical trends;

(4) current account flows were a fairly predictable function of relative prices and the relative cyclical position of the countries concerned; and

(5) short-term capital (or "hot money") was considered liable to move in an unpredictable way in response to speculative or interest rate factors.

In this view of the world, three types of dangers were perceived to be important. First, the volatility of short-term capital was thought likely to give rise to undesirable short-term fluctuations in exchange rates. (A related fear was that in the absence of short-term stabilizing speculation, individual large current account transactions might themselves introduce instability into day-to-day rates.) A second fear was that short-term swings in a country's balance of payments (for example, for seasonal reasons), might lead to unnecessary exchange rate shifts unless "buffered" by reserve changes. And a third fear was that longer-lasting swings in the current account position (caused, for example, by cyclical factors) might give rise to exchange rate movements that would subsequently have to be reversed. This could be particularly damaging if weakness in the domestic economy led to a strengthening of the current account and if, as was widely believed at the time, a strengthening of the current account tended to push up the exchange rate. Such exchange rate appreciation would exert a depressing effect on economic activity and tend to further unbalance relative cyclical positions.

---

[92] Executive Board Decision No. 4232–(74/67), in *Selected Decisions of the International Monetary Fund*.

The "Guidelines for the Management of Floating Exchange Rates" addressed each of these three concerns. The first guideline stated that members should intervene to prevent or moderate short-term (day-to-day and week-to-week) fluctuations in rates. The second guideline permitted members to act ("through intervention or otherwise") to moderate month-to-month and quarter-to-quarter movements. The third guideline dealt with target zones. If countries wished to establish target zones, or exchange rate "norms," for their currencies, they could do so, but would have to consult with the Fund. If a country did not establish a target zone, the Fund itself could find that its rate has moved outside the "range of reasonable estimates of the medium-term norm for that rate." It could then encourage the member either to permit the rate to move back toward the range, or to take action to moderate further divergences. A member would not be asked to resist strong market pressure, and it was accepted that "on occasion, the market view [of an exchange rate] may be more realistic than the official view...."

The central focus of the policy actions discussed in the guidelines was the exchange market. The "Commentary" that accompanied the guidelines gave the following definition of exchange rate policies.

> "'Action to influence an exchange rate' includes, besides exchange market intervention, other policies that exercise a temporary effect on the balance of payments and hence on exchange rates, and that have been adopted for that purpose. Such policies may take the form of official forward exchange market intervention, official borrowing or lending, capital restrictions, separate capital exchange markets, various types of fiscal intervention, and also monetary or interest rate policies. Monetary or interest rate policies adopted for demand management purposes or other policies adopted for purposes other than balance of payments purposes would not be regarded as action to influence the exchange rate."

The "Guidelines for the Management of Floating Exchange Rates" did not contain specific procedures for monitoring, or for the exercise of surveillance. The major countries published reserves information that permitted a judgment to be reached as to whether intervention was moderating month-to-month or quarter-to-quarter movements in rates. Confidential information was also provided to show how intervention was used to counteract short-term volatility. Concerning the third guideline, however, no country with a floating exchange rate chose to consult with the Fund concerning a medium-term target zone, nor did the Fund use its powers to find that a country's rate had moved outside the range of reasonable estimates of a medium-term norm.

## 1977 Document

Efforts to improve the implementation of the 1974 guidelines were effectively suspended in January 1976, with agreement in principle on a new Article IV at the Jamaica meeting of the Interim Committee of the Fund. This agreement emphasized the central importance of stable domestic policies in providing the basis for a stable international monetary system.[93] Thus, the obligations placed on members in the amended Article IV gave emphasis to the need to foster orderly underlying economic and financial conditions, and to direct policies toward the objective of fostering orderly economic growth with reasonable price stability. Members' obligations with respect to exchange rate policies were to "avoid manipulating exchange rates or the international monetary system" and to "follow exchange policies compatible" with their other obligations. The amended Articles left to the Executive Board the working out of "specific principles for the guidance of all members with respect to those policies."

## Global Economic Environment, 1977

The Executive Board began consideration of principles for the guidance of members' exchange rate policies shortly after the agreement reached at Jamaica. At that time, three years had elapsed since the end of fixed rates and the adoption of floating by most major currencies. These three years had been characterized by: a major international recession; a fourfold increase in oil prices; a major shift in payments balances on current account; a surge of inflation; and a considerable degree of variability in exchange rate relationships.

Of particular note was the extreme variability of inflation, both across countries and over time. In 1975, for example, the average rate of increase in the GNP deflator of the seven largest industrial countries was 10½ percent, with a range running from about 7 percent in the Federal Republic of Germany to 28 percent in the United Kingdom. Within countries, changes in inflation performance were also dramatic. In Japan, for example, inflation touched 26½ percent (at an annual rate) in the first half of 1975, but had fallen back to 6 percent by the first half of the following year. In the United Kingdom, inflation fell from some 32 percent in the first half of 1975 to 12½ percent in the first half of 1976.

Also noteworthy were the sharp shifts in balance of payments positions that accompanied the substantial

---

[93] See *IMF Survey* (Washington), Vol. 15 (January 19, 1976).

changes that were taking place in the international economic environment. The U.S. current account was in small surplus in 1973 and 1974, then moved into record surplus in 1975, before shifting back toward deficit in 1976. Japan, by contrast, was in substantial deficit on its current account in 1974 before swinging strongly back into surplus in 1976.

Reflecting these developments, exchange rates also moved substantially. The U.S. dollar depreciated by 13 percent in effective terms in the first seven months of 1973 then recovered by 12 percent in the ensuing six months. The currencies of countries affected by high inflation rates (especially the pound sterling and the Italian lira) exhibited a general tendency to depreciate through most of the early years of the floating period. The countries with relatively good inflation performances throughout this period (such as the Federal Republic of Germany and Switzerland) showed a general tendency to appreciate, though with interruptions of one or two quarters. The Japanese yen, after having appreciated up to early 1974, then fell sharply as price increases in Japan accelerated.

## Lessons of Early Experience With Floating

It is not easy to characterize the lessons which policymakers in 1976 felt had been learned from the early experience with floating. Nevertheless, certain conclusions relevant for the design of surveillance principles seem possible. Four are of particular importance.

First, it was recognized that it had become considerably more difficult to estimate the underlying current account balances associated with a particular pattern of exchange rates. This was partly because there was more uncertainty about what constituted "normal" cyclical positions and their determinants. It had become difficult to interpret indices of capital utilization, since part of the capital stock had been rendered obsolete by the increase in energy prices. Moreover, traditional notions of full employment had become unrealistic as a guide to normal employment levels over the standard business cycle. A further difficulty in estimating underlying current account balances was created by the sharp movements that had occurred in terms of trade and relative costs. Since these factors affected current account positons with uncertain and distributed lags, and since they had fluctuated substantially during the preceding several years, it was difficult to estimate the relevant elasticities for the medium and longer run.

Second, it was recognized that normal capital flows had become considerably harder to estimate. With the significant increase in the balance of payments surpluses of oil countries, the disposition of capital flows in the world economy became much more dependent on the portfolio allocation decisions of the major oil-exporting countries. Not only that, prospective capital flows depended to a substantial extent on how, and how quickly, the surpluses of oil exporters would be absorbed in higher imports. With this uncertainty about the prospective level of "normal" capital flows for the major industrial countries, the current account position that was associated with overall equilibrium was also uncertain.

Third, the role of expectations in influencing exchange market developments was increasingly apparent. These expectations related both to factors that affected the current account directly, and to developments that could have a more general effect on overall economic performance. Movements in oil prices, for example, could affect currency relationships among industrial countries depending on the relative extent to which such price changes were expected to affect their payments positions. And shifts in inflation prospects resulting, say, from wage bargaining agreements, could affect exchange rates before showing up in actual cost differentials.

Fourth, the early experience with floating appeared to be consistent with the view that relative price performance (both actual and prospective) was perhaps the most important single determinant of exchange rate developments, at least over the medium term. The countries with the best price performance (the Federal Republic of Germany and Switzerland) had consistently appreciating rates; those with the worst price performance (Italy and the United Kingdom) had experienced depreciation; and the country with the most volatile inflation (Japan) had appreciated during the period when its performance was better than average and had depreciated when its inflation rate rose above the average. (It should be noted, of course, that there were also substantial movements in exchange rates that could not be related to price developments.)

## Implications for Surveillance

If the above lessons were indeed those that could be drawn from the initial experience with a regime of floating rates, they carried the following implications for the design of surveillance principles: first, it would be hard, if not impossible, to base exchange rate principles on the concept of an agreed equilibrium exchange rate; second, instability in exchange rates was the result of instability in the surrounding economic environment; third, a major source of instability in the surrounding environment was high and volatile inflation.

For these reasons, neither the amended Article IV nor the surveillance document adopted subsequently, makes any reference to the concept of "normal" or equilibrium exchange rates. The basic philosophy of the amended Article IV is that members should follow stable domestic policies that contribute to "orderly" economic growth and reasonable price stability. Members are not expected to take specific actions with regard to exchange rate policies, but rather to avoid "manipulation" and to follow policies "compatible" with the other undertakings of Article IV. The expectation was that the restoration of stability in the domestic economies of member countries would be the main requirement for restoring better stability in the international exchange rate system more generally.

The amended Article IV provided, in Section 3(b), for the Executive Board to adopt "specific principles for the guidance of all members" with respect to their exchange rate policies. However, the "specific principles" contained in the surveillance document go little farther than the text of the Article itself. They provide for intervention to counter "disorderly" market conditions, and enjoin countries to take account in intervention of the interests of the country issuing the intervention currency, but otherwise simply repeat the obligation to avoid manipulation.

The fact that the main principle of exchange rate policies is the need to "avoid manipulation" carries two implications that are worthy of note. The first is that, in the absence of manipulation, the pursuit of the other obligations of Article IV (namely, the fostering of orderly underlying economic and financial conditions) is expected to lead to a broadly satisfactory outcome for the exchange rate. The second is that some guidance is needed to recognize the existence of manipulation.

Identifying "manipulation" occupied a considerable part of the time devoted by the Executive Board to the formulation of the surveillance document. It was recognized early on that a wide range of economic policies affected exchange rates. However, it was also realized that some limitation was needed on those policies that would be considered as "exchange rate policies" if the necessary focus was to be provided for the Fund's surveillance activities. Therefore, attention was directed to policies that had a rather direct impact on conditions in the foreign exchange market. (Other policies would be reviewed by the Fund under its obligation to "oversee" members' compliance with their obligations to foster orderly underlying conditions, rather than as an aspect per se of surveillance over exchange rate policies.)

It was also recognized at an early stage that policy actions that might constitute manipulation under one set of circumstances would not necessarily be manipulative under other circumstances. Early drafts of the surveillance document contained the implication that certain actions—such as prolonged one-way intervention, excessive borrowing or lending or abnormal current or capital controls—would be considered prima facie evidence of manipulation. Eventually, however, it was agreed that such developments should be no more than "pointers," to be taken into account by the Managing Director in reaching a judgment on whether the possibility of a need for discussion with a member existed. It was also agreed that in addition to the specific "pointers" that could indicate the need for discussion with a member, any behavior of the exchange rate that appeared to be unrelated to underlying economic and financial conditions could also create the basis for supplementary consultation.

In brief, the conclusion was that, while manipulation could not be defined in the abstract, it could be identified in specific cases. It was therefore envisaged that, with the accumulation of a body of experience, it would become clearer, both to the Fund and to its member countries, what constituted manipulation. This approach dictated the structure of the document that was eventually adopted. Since it was not possible to develop "specific principles for the guidance of members" that went much beyond the language of the Articles, an indication was needed as to how such guidance would evolve over time. Thus in the document the principles for the guidance of members, which are rather general, are accompanied by principles for the guidance of the Fund, which attempt to illustrate circumstances in which a dialogue about the appropriateness of exchange rate policies should occur. There is then a section on procedures which specifies how that dialogue should be conducted and concluded.

## Exchange Rate System Since 1977

### Changing Policy Issues

The main issues that have arisen in the working of the exchange rate system over the past nine years have differed somewhat from those that were foreseen at the time the surveillance document was adopted. First, manipulation of the kind envisaged in the document has not been a serious problem. Second, although much greater price stability has been restored among the major countries, shifts in exchange rates have been substantial. Third, capital flows have proved to be larger and more volatile than could have been foreseen in 1977. And lastly, the procedure that provides for additional or special consultations has not been invoked, so that no "case law" has been built up that could help make members' obligations in the field of exchange rate policies more specific. Each of these features warrants some elaboration.

For much of the period since 1977, although exchange rates were certainly strongly influenced by divergences in policy mix, major industrial countries did not seek to affect conditions in the foreign exchange market directly, other than in the context of the EMS. This choice reflected a number of factors, including the belief that market forces would be effective in bringing about an appropriate exchange rate, a recognition that the resources at the disposal of private market participants were much larger than those of the authorities, the view that sterilized intervention would have only a transitory influence on market conditions, and the belief that unsterilized intervention would require an undesirable loss of control over domestic monetary conditions. Nevertheless, intervention has been felt to be useful in certain circumstances, especially when the authorities have believed a particular pattern of rates to be sustained by artificial factors and to be unrelated to fundamental factors. Concerted intervention has occurred on a number of occasions since 1977, including November 1978, September 1984, February 1985, and most recently in the months following the September 1985 meeting of the Group of Five in New York. On these occasions, the intervention, being coordinated (or at least agreed) among the countries directly involved, has not involved policy conflicts and has been felt to be useful in influencing exchange rates in an appropriate direction.

The period since the mid-1970s has also witnessed a considerable reduction in inflationary pressures in industrial countries, and a narrowing in the dispersion of inflation rates about their mean level. In 1974–76, inflation had averaged 10 percent in the industrial countries as a group, with a standard deviation of 4½ percentage points about this rate. By 1984–85, the average inflation rate had fallen below 4 percent with a standard deviation of less than 3 percentage points. The convergence of inflation rates toward a lower level did not, however, bring about the expected reduction in exchange rate variability, whether exchange rate movements are measured in the short or longer term. Quarter-to-quarter movements in key exchange rate relationships were considerably greater in 1984–85 than they had been in 1975–76. Medium-term exchange rate swings have also had greater amplitude. This is particularly evident for the U.S. dollar, whose real effective exchange rate (measured as a quarterly average) fluctuated within a range of 10 percent during 1974–76, but moved by more than 50 percent during the four years to the first quarter of 1985. There have also been striking movements in the exchange rates of other major currencies. The real effective rate of the Japanese yen, for example, fell by over 25 percent between late 1978 and early 1980, and the deutsche mark depreciated by a similar amount over the five years to early 1985. In both cases, the exchange rate movements were significantly larger than those that occurred in the first four years of floating.

One of the reasons for these unexpectedly wide movements in key exchange rates is to be found in the growing importance of divergences in the economic policy mix in creating incentives for capital flows. While it has been recognized for some time that the foreign exchange market should be viewed largely as an asset market, it was generally felt that the determinants of market participants' willingness to hold assets in different currencies would be affected by many of the same factors that influenced the evolution of current account positions. It has become clear, however, that the volume of internationally mobile capital is sufficient to finance current account imbalances that are considerably larger and more prolonged than was earlier considered possible.

The fact that "manipulation" has rarely occurred, at least in the restrictive sense envisaged in the surveillance document, has meant that the specific provisions for supplemental consultations have not been invoked. The realization that it would be difficult for the Managing Director of the Fund to initiate special discussions under the surveillance decision, because it would be interpreted as overt disagreement with a member's policies, gave rise to the 1979 decision on supplemental surveillance procedures. These were intended to provide a neutral basis for discussions, by permitting consultations to take place following any exchange rate development that "may be important or may have important effects on other members."[94]

## Weaknesses in Working of Exchange Rate System

The features of the international economic environment described above have led to three kinds of development that are of concern from the point of view of the international exchange rate system. First, short-term exchange rate volatility among major currencies has created a climate of uncertainty that has been felt to impede the balanced expansion of trade and investment. Second, medium-term exchange rate swings of these currencies have been associated with a balance of payments structure that cannot be considered sustainable in a longer-term context. And third, many countries with fixed exchange rates have devel-

---

[94] Decision No. 6026–(79/13), *Selected Decisions of the International Monetary Fund*, p. 15.

oped unsustainable current account deficits, financed by excessive borrowing from commercial sources. Such overborrowing culminated in the debt crisis when access to capital inflows was curtailed. These concerns may be considered in turn.

Short-term exchange rate volatility became much larger after the advent of generalized floating and, contrary to some expectations, has not shown any tendency to diminish with the passage of time. The average of daily changes in the rates of five major currencies against the U.S. dollar, which had been well under 0.1 percent during the decade of the 1960s, averaged 0.3 percent during 1974–76, and was 0.5 percent in 1983–85. A similar picture emerges when monthly rates are considered. Average movements in monthly average exchange rates were around 0.1 percent in the 1960s, 1.6 percent in 1974–76, and 2.4 percent in 1983–85.

However, while this volatility undoubtedly introduces an additional degree of uncertainty into the finance of international trade, neither a priori reasoning nor empirical evidence suggests that the effects of short-term exchange rate movements on the volume of international trade have been substantial. Well-developed forward markets exist for short-term maturities in all major currencies, and the cost of purchasing forward cover in these markets (measured as the spread between bid and offer prices) remains small. It is true that forward markets are less available for the currencies of developing countries, but this cannot be attributed mainly to the volatility of rates among major currencies. With relatively few exceptions, empirical studies of the effects of short-term exchange rate volatility on trade have concluded that there is little evidence to support the contention that such effects are of major importance.[95]

The same cannot be said of the longer-lasting swings in exchange rates that have also characterized the floating rate period. Such exchange rate movements, unlike the short-term volatility discussed above, do last long enough to affect resource allocation decisions. They give rise to shifts in profitability that can induce major reallocations of resources between traded and nontraded goods industries. The prospect of such profitability shifts can reduce the attractiveness of capital formation (particularly in longer-lived assets). When relative costs do change, unemployment can result, as well as the direct costs involved in transferring resources to new activities. Moreover, when unemployment appears to be due to the capricious behavior of the foreign exchange market, it can more easily generate pressures for protectionism. Lastly, when large exchange rate movements are associated with the buildup of unsustainable current account imbalances, uncertainty is created about when and how the eventual reversal of these imbalances will be brought about.

The third concern about the functioning of the exchange rate system relates not to the variability of exchange rates in industrial countries but to the way in which developing countries have been able to use excessive external borrowing to delay needed balance of payments adjustment. The size of resulting imbalances financed through reliance on unsustainable capital inflows in the period leading up to 1982 meant that the loss of creditworthiness that occurred in that year had more severe consequences for the economies concerned than need otherwise have been the case. The responsibility for the crisis that emerged in 1982 must be shared by countries which over-borrowed, creditors which over-lent, and the institutional arrangements that permitted such developments to occur. In the three years 1979–81, the group of countries which later experienced debt-servicing difficulties increased their borrowing from commercial banks at an average annual rate of 24 percent. In 1984–85, their net borrowing grew at a rate of only 2 percent, and would have shrunk by a substantial amount had it not been for major packages of concerted lending under rescheduling arrangements. With the benefit of hindsight, it is possible to see that these countries were enabled to maintain unsustainable exchange rate and current account positions through excessive official borrowing—even though such borrowing was not specifically undertaken for balance of payments purposes.

## Implications for Surveillance Principles

The foregoing discussion carries a number of important implications for the design of principles for the conduct of members' exchange rate policies. Six seem particularly worthy of note.

(1) The absence of manipulation is a necessary, but not a sufficient, condition for the emergence of a satisfactory underlying balance of payments position. There have been few instances, if any, where major countries have for balance of payments purposes adopted policies that could reasonably be said to hamper the working of the adjustment process. Yet there has been considerable volatility in exchange

---

[95] See International Monetary Fund, *Exchange Rate Volatility and World Trade*, Occasional Paper No. 28 (Washington, July 1986); M.A. Akhtar and R.S. Hilton, "Exchange Rate Uncertainties and International Trade," Research Paper No. 8403 (New York, Federal Reserve Bank of New York, May 1984); and Padma Gotur, "Effects of Exchange Rate Volatility on Trade: Some Further Evidence," *Staff Papers*, International Monetary Fund (Washington), Vol. 32 (September 1985), pp. 475–512.

rates, and currency values have moved to levels that proved unsustainable in the longer run.

(2) The restoration of domestic price stability is not in itself sufficient to restore exchange rate stability. This result is contrary to a number of expectations that were entertained at the time the surveillance document was adopted. At that time, the high level of inflation, and the prevailing uncertainty about future price trends, were considered to be the major factors behind the unexpected degree of exchange rate variability in the early years of floating. In recent years, however, the average rate of inflation has fallen dramatically, and the dispersion of price increases has narrowed, but the amplitude of exchange rate swings has increased.

(3) The principal determinants of medium-term exchange rate swings in industrial countries are fluctuations in domestic saving/investment balances. These induce capital flows which in turn give rise to exchange rate movements and generate the shift in current account positions that is the counterpart of the change in domestic saving/investment balances. Thus, if it is desired to diminish the amplitude of exchange rate movements, actions must be taken to stabilize saving/investment balances.

(4) Government policies, and in particular the mix of monetary and fiscal policy, are a major determinant of shifts in national saving and investment levels. At the same time, the effectiveness of policy in promoting an environment that is conducive to saving and investment in the private sector can also be important. These policies have not thus far been framed with exchange rate objectives in mind, but exchange rate considerations would need to become more important if exchange rate stability were to be accorded greater priority as a policy objective.

(5) The current principles for the guidance of members' exchange rate policies do not, by themselves, provide sufficient guidance to generate medium-term exchange rate stability. Since the choice of policy mix through which members seek to create "orderly domestic economic and financial conditions" is left to the individual member, it is possible for divergent choices to lead to undesired exchange rate patterns. The procedures that exist for policy mixes to be discussed are useful but fall short of being a mechanism for effective reconciliation of policy objectives.

(6) The role of intervention in exchange rate management is a limited one. Experience has led the major countries to the conclusion that sterilized intervention cannot have a major or lasting impact on the exchange rate determined by fundamental economic factors.[96] It is recognized, however, that intervention can be helpful on occasions where market exchange rates appear to have diverged from the pattern implied by economic fundamentals, or when the authorities wish to communicate to the market their determination to pursue a particular policy course with respect to fundamentals.

## Possible Modifications in Surveillance

### Some Objectives

The fundamental objective of the Fund's activities in the field of surveillance remains the efficient operation of the international monetary system. This purpose is stated clearly at the outset of Article IV: ". . . the essential purpose of the international monetary system is to provide a framework that facilitates the exchange of goods, services and capital among countries, and that sustains sound economic growth. . ."

The language of Article IV goes on to state that a principal objective is the development of orderly underlying conditions, and requires members to collaborate with the Fund and other members to assure orderly exchange arrangements and promote a stable system of exchange rates. All these purposes remain equally valid in today's circumstances, as do the objectives of promoting economic growth and reasonable price stability and avoiding harmful manipulation of exchange rates.

Nevertheless, it can be argued that the individual pursuit of these objectives by member countries has not been as successful as could be hoped in promoting "a framework that facilitates the exchange of goods, services and capital among countries, and that sustains sound economic growth," and has been unsuccessful in promoting a stable system of exchange rates. Long-term exchange rate variability has created damaging uncertainties, and wide fluctuations in flows of funds between countries have required costly reallocation of resources. Moreover, the weakness of the surveillance mechanism and the way capital flows have operated helped to precipitate the debt-servicing crisis from which the world economy is still recovering.

It is widely agreed that the correction of these deficiencies in the functioning of the international monetary system should be an important objective of policy. Efforts in this direction can follow two approaches (which are not mutually exclusive): (1) the guidance given to member countries and to the Fund itself through decisions of the Executive Board can be amended; and (2) the manner in which guidance is implemented can be improved. Since it has been argued in this paper that the principles set forth in the

---

[96] See "Report of the Working Group on Exchange Market Intervention" (chaired by P. Jurgensen), January 1983.

surveillance document remain valid, any amendment to the existing language would presumably be to clarify, extend, or make more specific the guidance given to members with respect to their exchange rate policies. Amendments could also be made so as to indicate more precisely circumstances in which the Fund would be expected to invoke the consultation procedures provided for in the document.

Before proceeding to a discussion of the changes in the surveillance document that could be suggested by the proposals made in the Group of Ten and Group of Twenty-Four Reports, it is useful to have a clear idea of the structure and scope of the 1977 decision. The document itself contains four sections. The first, entitled "General Principles," defines the limits of the document: it underlines its objective to deal only with the topic of exchange rate policies. The second section of the document provides principles for the guidance of members. The third section sets forth principles to guide the Fund in its exercise of surveillance over members' exchange rate policies. And the fourth section provides for certain procedures to be followed, pertaining both to multilateral and to bilateral review of exchange rate policies. In addition to the provisions contained in the document, an Executive Board Decision of 1979 (No. 6026-(79/13)) provides for supplemental surveillance procedures, and the periodic reviews of the implementation of surveillance have led to a number of developments in practice.

## General Principles

The section of the document entitled "General Principles" defines the scope of the document as a whole. It limits the coverage of the principles and procedures to exchange rate policies, thus excluding domestic economic policies (regarding which the Fund also has oversight responsibilities under Article IV, Section 3(a)). It is recognized that there is a close relationship between domestic and international economic policies, although the language of the document does not indicate how this relationship should be taken account of by the Fund in the exercise of its surveillance responsibilities.

The key issue in connection with the general principles is whether the surveillance that the Fund is called on to exercise over exchange rate policies should involve examination of members' compliance with the obligations covered in Section 1 of Article IV, regarding the objective of fostering stable economic and financial conditions and a monetary system that does not tend to produce erratic disruptions. The justification for such an extension would be the increasing recognition that exchange rate movements that cause international concern are more often the unintended result of divergences and inadequacies in domestic policies rather than the deliberate consequences of policies aimed at influencing conditions in the foreign exchange market. It is clear from Article IV, Section 1, that members have obligations in the field of domestic economic policies, in particular, the obligation of seeking to promote stability and fostering orderly underlying economic and financial conditions. Under Article IV, Section 3(a), the Fund has a duty to oversee the compliance of each member with these obligations. Of course, the Articles do not give the Fund powers of surveillance in areas where members' policies do not affect the interests of other members. Judgment is therefore necessary in deciding where the line should be drawn. Nevertheless, the experience of recent years is abundantly clear: domestic policies and their international interaction *do* have an impact on exchange rates and on the stability of the system. To be effective, surveillance must be extended to all policies having such effects.

## Principles for Guidance of Members' Exchange Rate Policies

The section "Principles for the Guidance of Members' Exchange Rate Policies" contains three principles. Two relate to short-term intervention to counter disorderly market conditions and, being uncontroversial, need not be considered further here. The other guidance provided is a repetition of the obligation, in Article IV, to avoid manipulation of exchange rates or the international monetary system in order to prevent effective balance of payments adjustment or to gain an unfair competitive advantage over other members. The rather general nature of this language has the advantage of flexibility, since it permits judgment to be exercised according to the circumstances of individual cases. It has the drawback, however, of providing relatively little concrete guidance, and permitting conflicting interpretations. As events have shown, such guidance has not in practice prevented the emergence of exchange rate swings that have created international concerns. If it were felt desirable to introduce more specific guidance, the possible approaches would fall under three main headings:

(1) Countries could be encouraged to establish limits to the zone of fluctuations for their currency, and to undertake certain actions, or at least to consult, as the value of their currency moved outside the zone.

(2) Countries could be encouraged to establish limits on the development of certain domestic policy variables which, together with guidance covering interven-

tion in the foreign exchange market, would be presumed to help establish a "sustainable" exchange rate.

(3) The kind of behavior that constitutes manipulation, and that is therefore proscribed, could be more precisely and meaningfully defined. Such a definition would presumably extend beyond actions narrowly directed at the exchange market.

If none of these approaches were to meet with favor, a fourth approach would be to retain the present rather general guidelines, and to focus on procedural mechanisms for improving policy formulation and coordination.

Each of the suggestions just noted can be found, explicitly or implicitly, in either the Group of Ten or the Group of Twenty-Four Report. As noted in chapter 1, the Group of Twenty-Four Report favors target zones for the major currencies on the grounds that this would help achieve the objective of exchange rate stability and sustainable levels of payments balances. The Group of Ten Report, by contrast, opposes the establishment of a target zone system (with some Deputies dissenting). The principal reasons given are that it would prove extremely difficult in practice to reach a consensus on the range of desirable exchange rates, that market behavior that was inconsistent with zones would add to instability, and that the constraints on domestic policies imposed by target zones might undermine efforts to pursue sound and stable policies in the medium term.

The adoption of some variant of the target zone proposal as the basis for the operation of the exchange rate system would have clear implications for the principles and implementation of Fund surveillance over exchange rate policies. Among the issues that would need to be decided are the following: (1) should the adoption of target zones be mandatory or optional? (Mandatory target zones would of course require amendment of the Articles, since the existing Articles give members freedom, subject to certain limitations, to maintain exchange arrangements of their choice); (2) in what forum would a multilateral grid of rates or zones for the largest currencies be decided?; (3) how wide should target zones be?; (4) what procedures should be applied for changing target zones?; (5) what undertakings would countries make with respect to zones? (Should they undertake to act to prevent their currencies moving outside the zone or simply to consult with respect to the reasons for the departure?); and (6) Should target zones be publicly announced or rather used as a basis for confidential discussions among the countries concerned?

The issue of undertakings with respect to target zones raises a further series of questions concerning the nature of the guidance to be given, through surveillance principles, to members and to the Fund. For example, if it were felt that members should act to prevent currencies moving outside target zones (or to limit the extent of such a movement) should the principles for the guidance of members' policies specify the type of policies that can be employed for this purpose? This could be done with varying degrees of precision. At one extreme, there could be an undertaking analogous to that of the Bretton Woods system to intervene in exchange markets to prevent any departure from the established zones. Then, if countries wished to avoid undesired monetary consequences from such interventions, they would have to take steps to ensure that other economic policy instruments were deployed in a manner consistent with the commitment to the exchange rate zone. Alternatively, the guidance given to countries could be somewhat looser, involving either encouragement to take action that would move the currency back inside the zone, or to abstain from actions of a kind that would lead to a further departure. Even more loosely, the undertaking could simply be one of consulting with the Fund, which would then raise questions concerning how such consultation would proceed, and how disagreements would be resolved. These questions would have to be dealt with under the section of the surveillance document that deals with procedures (see below).

The possibility of establishing indicators covering domestic policy performance is mentioned in the Report of the Group of Ten. This proposal has at its base the view that undesirable exchange rate variability is mainly the result of inappropriate domestic policies, and that any attempt to promote more stable exchange rates should focus directly on national policy formation. There has been relatively little discussion, in either official or academic circles, of what form such "domestic policy-oriented targets" might take.[97] Questions exist concerning (1) whether such targets should be expressed in terms of policy outcomes or policy instruments; (2) how wide a range of policy outcomes or instruments should be subject to targets; (3) how such policies might be quantified; (4) how agreement could be reached on appropriate targets or zones; and (5) what action would be called for in the event that the targets were not adhered to.

Despite the importance of promoting satisfactory and convergent economic performance, there are some practical difficulties in basing surveillance on undertakings with respect to economic outcomes (such as, for example, economic growth or the rate of inflation). Economic outcomes can certainly be influenced by the

---

[97] For a discussion of these issues, see "Review and Assessment of the System of Floating Exchange Rates," chapter I of this Occasional Paper.

authorities through policy instruments, but they are also subject to unexpected exogenous developments. From a practical viewpoint, therefore, there would be advantages in confining domestic economic targets to the setting of policy instruments. The key issue is which instruments should be subject to such control. It seems clear that the aggregate stance of domestic fiscal and monetary policies is an important element in overall economic and financial policies, and therefore should be a part of any such targets that are arrived at. However, it could also be argued that structural policies are important in creating exchange rate movements. Countries that are unsuccessful in removing structural rigidities are likely to experience difficulties in preventing capital outflows, and thus may experience a depreciation in the value of their currency relative to that of countries where superior economic performance tends to attract capital inflows.

When it comes to quantifying domestic macroeconomic policies, the most widely used indicators are some measure of growth in the domestic money supply, and an indicator of the size of the government's fiscal deficit. Judgment would have to be exercised, however, in picking a precise measure for these variables. Most of the large industrial countries use several different measures of the money supply as a means of monitoring the evolution of monetary policy. These measures can move in a somewhat different manner, particularly over short periods. Moreover, the behavior of the demand for money, and thus the appropriate path for the money stock, can be influenced by developments such as financial innovation and changes in the regulatory environment. For these reasons, several major countries have adopted an eclectic approach to the assessment of monetary conditions, involving attention to a variety of financial indicators. With regard to fiscal policy, there is a similar variety of possible indicators. The fiscal deficit or surplus can be measured at the central or general government level, and can be adjusted for cyclical factors or left unadjusted. There is also the possibility of adjustment for other factors of a systematic nature (such as inflation) or of a more ad hoc nature (large nonrecurring transactions, for example). Lastly, other types of fiscal indicator could include the level of government expenditure, and the level and incidence of taxation. The variety of possible measures of the fiscal and monetary stance complicates the task of developing meaningful and comparable indicators of domestic policy stance, but it need not make it impossible, provided adequate flexibility is employed in expressing objectives with respect to these policies. For example, zones rather than specific targets could be established, or undertakings could be expressed in terms of the avoidance of large (or sudden, or disruptive) changes in the chosen measure.

With regard to the issue of how to give operational content to domestic policy undertakings, several possibilities exist. Members could be called upon to set out quantified objectives for monetary and fiscal policies for a given period ahead. This could occur at the time of an Article IV consultation and be subject to review by (or the concurrence of) the Executive Board. Deviations from expressed objectives, as endorsed by the Board, could then be a trigger for a review by the Board of the circumstances in which the deviation had occurred. An alternative would be to express countries' undertakings more loosely as being to avoid sudden disruptive shifts in monetary and fiscal policies, or to formulate such policies so as to promote the efficient working of the adjustment process. The Fund would then have to exercise judgment, during Article IV consultations and at other times, about whether actual policies were consistent with the guidance that had been given.

In assessing what consequences should follow from any departure from the expressed objectives of monetary and fiscal policies, it would have to be recognized that deviations from targets could occur for a variety of reasons. For example, an unexpected shift in velocity could render a previously existing money supply target unrealistic. In the field of fiscal policy, a target for the central government borrowing requirement might be missed because of unexpected weakness (or strength) in economic activity. Given the variety of circumstances which could cause a deviation from domestic policy targets, it would not be wise to prescribe too closely the response called for in such circumstances. One possibility would be to simply provide for consultation with the Fund. This would permit the country concerned to explain its perception of the causes of the developments that had occurred, and other countries to express any concerns they might feel; it would not bind the member to a particular course of action. Another possibility would be to call upon the member not to undertake discretionary action that would cause a further deviation of the policy instrument from its target until consultation with (and/or the concurrence of) the Fund had occurred.

The third broad approach, noted above, to changing the "Principles for Guidance of Members' Exchange Rate Policies," would be to introduce greater specificity into the description of policies that are to be avoided. This approach had been attempted in the early stages of drafting the 1977 document, when it was suggested that certain kinds of foreign exchange market actions, such as large-scale direct intervention, official borrowing or lending, or the use of controls, could create a presumption that "manipulation" was occurring. In the event, this approach did not meet with favor, as it was felt that the kinds of actions described could be desirable in certain circumstances and it would not be justified to create any presumption about their appropriateness. It was seen, furthermore, as involving an element of discriminatory treatment, as countries with floating exchange rates were less likely to find themselves intervening in exchange markets than countries with fixed rates.

Now that more experience has been gained with the operation of the current exchange rate system, it is possible to identify certain types of policy that have led to difficulties in the operation of the adjustment process. For example, divergences in the fiscal/monetary mix among major industrial countries have led at times to patterns of exchange rates and current account balances that could not be considered sustainable over the longer term. And heavy borrowing by a number of developing countries in the period up to 1982 led to a crisis situation when less favorable prospects for export market growth and the future course of real interest rates caused a reappraisal of creditworthiness. In both cases, problems arose because capital flows were allowed or encouraged to continue to a point where they affected adversely the efficient working of the adjustment process. It would be possible for the "Principles for the Guidance of Members' . . ." to include provisions encouraging countries to avoid policies that led to such results. Such provisions could be couched with varying degrees of specificity. If it were difficult to reach agreement on the precise nature of policy actions to be avoided, it could be provided that members should avoid measures that were inconsistent with the goal of promoting balance of payments adjustment in the medium term. This would require judgments to be reached concerning the type of policies needed for effective adjustment, which could perhaps be adapted from appraisals made during the course of Article IV consultations.

## Principles of Fund Surveillance Over Exchange Rate Policies

This section of the surveillance document is a list of developments "which might indicate the need for discussion with a member." As noted earlier, the section evolved out of an attempt to develop a list that would create the presumption of manipulation; the hesitant tone of the language eventually agreed reflected the wish of the Board not to create such a presumption in the finally agreed wording. Nevertheless, the purpose of the section is to give some guidance to the Fund in how to judge whether a member has (or might have) acted inconsistently with the guidance provided in the previous section.

The first such indicator is protracted large-scale exchange market intervention in one direction. The next three indicators are the use, for balance of payments purposes, of current or capital controls, external borrowing and lending, or monetary and other financial policies. The last indicator is "behavior of the exchange rate that appears to be unrelated to underlying economic and financial conditions. . . ."

A first issue in relation to the continuing appropriateness of these indicators is whether it remains sufficient to limit the indicators described to actions undertaken "for balance of payments purposes." The section does state, in a later paragraph, that any appraisal by the Fund should take place within the framework of a comprehensive analysis of the general economic situation and economic policy strategy of the member, and should recognize that domestic as well as external policies can contribute to timely adjustment of the balance of payments. Nevertheless, the deletion of the proviso "for balance of payments purposes" from some of the policy developments listed in the section could help broaden the scope of the Fund's responsibilty. For example, large-scale official borrowing by heavily indebted countries contributed to the subsequent emergence of the debt crisis, but it could be argued that such borrowing was not specifically undertaken "for balance of payments purposes." Equally, the large capital flows among industrial countries that produced large exchange rate movements resulted from policies that were not primarily oriented to balance of payments objectives. The fact that inappropriate policies are not undertaken specifically for balance of payments purposes does not, of course, prevent the Fund from expressing its views on them during the course of the consultation process.

A second issue relates to the possibility of extending the list of indicators, or making it more precise. Since, as noted above, unsustainable capital flows have been a major source of subsequent difficulties in the international economic system, the emergence of such flows could be used as an additional explicit indicator of the need for special consultations. Other possible additions to the list of indicators would depend, to a considerable extent, on the outcome of decisions with respect to the principles for the guidance of members' policies. The Managing Director of the Fund should presumably be directed to initiate discussions in circumstances where principles established for members' policies have not been observed.

A final issue covers the degree of judgment to be exercised by the Managing Director in initiating discussions under the surveillance decision. Since the exchange rate developments listed under the "Principles of Fund Surveillance" are not defined precisely, and in any event are only to be considered as indicators, considerable judgment remains with the Managing

Director, although he is required to "[take] into account any views that may have been expressed by other members." One consequence of this is that the formal procedures (see below) for initiating a special consultation under Article IV, Section 3(b), have never been invoked (although informal contacts have been held on a number of occasions). A rather more specific set of guidelines for Fund action would make the surveillance procedures somewhat more automatic.

## Procedures

Surveillance procedures of different kinds are provided for in the 1977 document, and in subsequent decisions of the Executive Board.

(1) The 1977 document provides for "regular" consultations between the Fund and member countries under Article IV. These consultations are to include both the observance by members of specific principles with respect to exchange rate policies, and obligations under Article IV, Section 1.

(2) The document provides for the continuation of periodic reviews of exchange rate developments within the framework of the World Economic Outlook exercise.

(3) The document provides for special procedures to be invoked if the Managing Director believes, in the interval between Article IV consultations, a member's policies may not be in accord with the exchange rate principles.

(4) A decision on supplemental surveillance procedures, adopted in January 1979, provides for consultations to take place in certain circumstances where important exchange rate developments have occurred, but no presumption exists that the exchange rate principles have not been observed.

(5) Beginning in 1983 (Decision No. 7374–(83/55, 3/28/83)) the staff has provided quarterly reports on indicators of real effective exchange rates and has issued "Information Notices" when the real effective exchange rate for an individual currency moves by more than 10 percent from the date of the last consultation.

A number of the procedural proposals made in the Group of Ten and Group of Twenty-Four Reports relate to the way in which the procedures just described are implemented. As such, their adoption would not require any change in the basic surveillance document. Other proposals would, however, require changes, either in the text of the procedures section of the 1977 surveillance document, or in the 1979 decision establishing the supplemental procedure.

Perhaps the key aspect of any modification to existing decisions concerns the degree of discretion the Managing Director is called upon to exercise in invoking specific consultations. It can be argued that such discretion provides a desirable element of judgment in the assessment of whether a particular exchange rate development requires further investigation. On the other hand, experience suggests that the Managing Director may find it invidious to single out countries for special discussions, and thus special or supplemental consultations at the level of the Executive Board may not take place. The Group of Ten Deputies noted that "it could be helpful if the IMF made greater use of supplemental surveillance procedures" and the Group of Twenty-Four Report made a similar suggestion in almost identical language.

The adoption of target zones for exchange rates, or "indicators" for domestic policy variables, would provide an automatic trigger for the review of a member's policies by the Fund. The procedural issues that would arise would be those related to how to proceed once such a review had been set in train. Specifically, should the exercise of "peer pressure" during the review process, as suggested by the Group of Ten, be the main sanction at the disposal of the Fund, or should other steps be envisaged. Additional steps could involve, for example, a finding by the Fund that a member's policies were inconsistent with the guidance given under the surveillance decision.

If target zones or policy indicators were not in existence, other means would have to be sought to trigger a review by the Fund of a member's policies. It might be possible to specify that, when a member's policies departed from those found by the Executive Board to be appropriate on the occasion of the last Article IV consultation, as expressed in the Chairman's summing up, the Managing Director should be required to bring such a departure to the attention of the Executive Board, either through an information notice, or through the tabling of a paper for the agenda. An alternative would be to retain the present system of information notices (perhaps with a different threshold of exchange rate movement) and to provide for more automatic discussion. For example, the staff could be required to make an appraisal in each information notice of whether the exchange rate change described in it was of a kind likely to promote the working of the adjustment process. Where such a statement could not be made on the basis of the information available to the staff, it could be provided that a Board meeting would automatically ensue. Care would need to be taken, however, to avoid a proliferation of meetings on exchange rate developments of marginal significance.

# III  Indicators of Policies and Economic Performance

The year 1986 saw a growing interest in the potential uses of objective indicators for monitoring international economic interactions and facilitating the coordination of economic policies. For example, both the April 1986 Interim Committee Communiqué and the May 1986 Tokyo Economic Declaration contained references to the role of indicators in the process of multilateral surveillance. Among variables specifically mentioned in this connection were: GNP growth rates, inflation rates, interest rates, unemployment rates, fiscal deficit ratios, current account and trade balances, monetary growth rates, reserves, and exchange rates.

This chapter considers a number of theoretical and practical aspects of the use of indicators in analyzing economic policies and performance. It begins by assessing the purposes that indicators might be expected to serve. The following section presents an analytical framework for discussing policy interactions among countries. Next, some suggestions are offered concerning the nature of the specific indicators that might be helpful in this connection, and the analysis concludes with a summary of some of the main issues that need to be resolved.

It may be helpful to note at the outset certain restrictions that have been placed on the scope of the discussion. First, it is preliminary in nature: it describes an approach to the use of indicators, but it does not attempt to apply the approach. Second, the analysis is developed with the larger industrial countries in mind. This reflects the fact that the large countries have the greatest impact on global economic conditions. Moreover, if indicators are to be discussed from the perspective of international interactions, there is a practical limit to the number of countries that can be covered in an initial assessment. Nevertheless, many of the principles and issues that are discussed have applications for countries outside the major industrial group. Third, no attempt is made to develop new or unfamiliar indicators. This is largely because the range of indicators that are customarily used in analysis seems broad enough to meet the needs of a more intensified assessment of international interactions of policies and performance. Moreover, since the objective is to develop an analytical framework that enables issues of coordination to be viewed in a fresh perspective, it is desirable not to burden the analysis with unnecessary complexity in the choice of variables to be employed.

## Purpose of Indicators

The use of indicators in the assessment of economic performance has a long history, both in the Fund and elsewhere. Their basic purpose is to give quantitative content to governments' economic aims and achievements, both in the realm of policies and performance. Indicators can thereby be used as a guide in helping judge the realism and appropriateness of objectives, and their consistency with international goals such as efficient adjustment, stability in trade flows, and sustainability of capital movements.[98] They can also be used to publicize governments' commitments to a particular course of policy, and thus to improve the basis for private sector decision taking.

The recent statements of the Interim Committee and the Summit participants, as well as the earlier reports of the Group of Ten and Group of Twenty-Four,[99] suggest at least three ways in which existing uses of indicators might be extended: (1) through a more explicit focus on the international repercussions of developments in individual countries; (2) by casting objectives and policies into a medium-term framework; and (3) by the development of standards against which developments in the various indicators can be appraised.

Indicators can be used both ex ante, in formulating objectives, policies and projections, as well as ex post, in monitoring progress toward desired objectives. In a forward-looking sense, indicators can help define a government's economic objectives and the policies through which it hopes to achieve those objectives.

---

[98] A report prepared for the Committee of Twenty by the Technical Group on Indicators discussed a number of technical problems concerning indicators in the adjustment process. (See "Documents of the Committee of Twenty" (Washington: International Monetary Fund, 1974), pp. 51–77.)

[99] See Appendices I and II.

Economic objectives include variables such as output, employment, and balance of payments and price stability. The policies which are available to foster these objectives include: fiscal policy, that is, the level and structure of government revenues and expenditures; monetary policy, or the rate of growth of monetary and credit aggregates and the setting of other monetary instruments; and structural policies, such as the degree of regulation in particular industries and markets. There are, in addition, intermediate variables that are neither ultimate goals of policy nor direct policy instruments, but which nevertheless have an important bearing on the interaction of policies among countries. These variables include real and nominal interest rates, exchange rates, and the relative growth rates of domestic saving and investment. Normally countries will have expectations or forecasts of how such variables might evolve, based on their assumptions about the channels through which policies work to influence the outcome for broader economic objectives.

A second way in which indicators can be used is in a retrospective or monitoring sense. Indicators can define how an economy has performed in some past period, and what the stance of policies has been. Used in this way, however, they need to be complemented by some standard, or frame of reference, against which to judge whether policies have been appropriate and performance has been successful. Such a standard can be the set of indicators and projections formulated at the outset of a policy period. It has to be recognized, however, that when an expected time path is specified for a large number of interconnected variables, some indicators may show deviations while others remain on track. A framework is therefore required for judging the significance, in particular circumstances, of departures from expected developments.

Both of the purposes of indicators that have just been described can be (and often have been) used in a purely national context without reference to international interactions. However, indicators can also be used for purposes of assessing the intercountry consistency of developments and prospects. In the framework of surveillance, this is likely to be an aspect of indicators that assumes increasing importance. Two kinds of consistency are important from an international standpoint: first, the projections being made by individual countries should be arithmetically consistent with those of other countries, for example, with respect to anticipated rates of growth of exports and imports. Second, and more fundamentally, projected developments should be compatible with the medium-term objectives of a stable system. These objectives would include sustainable balance of payments positions, combined with satisfactory performance with respect to growth and inflation.

To be effective in serving the purposes of analyzing and interpreting developments, economic indicators must be timely, quantifiable, relatively easy to interpret, and adequately comparable, both across countries and in relation to objective standards. It has to be recognized of course, that few indicators will be satisfactory in all these respects. In particular, single-valued indicators do not generally capture the complexity of the economic situation they are being used to portray. Most economic variables, for example, reflect a combination of underlying and persistent influences, as well as transitory phenomena. It is important in analysis to distinguish between such influences, so that responses are not triggered to developments that eventually prove self reversing. Thus, while tractability requires a limited number of relatively straightforward indicators, it should be recognized that additional analysis will usually be needed to provide an adequately rounded picture of economic developments, policies, and prospects.

## An Analytical Framework

As noted in the Interim Committee Communiqué, a key objective of the use of indicators in surveillance is to "strengthen the basis for assessing the international repercussions of the policies and objectives of the major industrial countries, and also to help promote the further development of recent initiatives to enhance policy coordination. . . ." Against this background, it seems appropriate to focus explicitly on how developments in the policies and economic performance of individual major countries influence the opportunities and constraints faced by other industrial countries, and the international community at large.

The principal point of interaction between national economies is trade and capital flows. These flows are influenced by the level and structure of demand growth in the various countries, by relative expected rates of return on assets, and by relative national price levels adjusted for exchange rates. The role of multilateral surveillance is to help countries move toward better and more consistent developments for all these variables. Indicators can assist in this process by providing a framework in which the evolution of policies and economic performance can be measured against their desired or expected path.

All countries have, as ultimate economic objectives, an optimal rate of utilization of existing factors of production, satisfactory growth of output over time, and reasonable price stability. However, the achievement of these objectives will be significantly affected by developments in the external sector. Trade in goods and services can help bring about a more efficient allocation of global resources, as countries concentrate production in industries in which they have a comparative advantage. Capital flows can help improve the volume and distribution of international investment, since they permit flows of real resources from countries where savings exceed investment opportunities to countries where the reverse prevails.

The potential benefits of international trade and investment flows can be reduced, however, when policies and developments among countries are inadequately harmonized. Inappropriate or uncoordinated national policies can lead to trade and capital flows that do not reflect comparative advantage or relative scarcities. Such flows, in turn, can generate volatility and uncertainty concerning the future path of interest rates, exchange rates, and payments flows. Added costs may be incurred when resources have to be shifted back and forth between uses in response to unnecessary or reversible changes in competitive conditions. Lastly, and perhaps most important, protectionist pressures can be created when international trade is perceived to be influenced by factors that seem to be unrelated to more fundamental supply and demand considerations.

In analyzing economic interactions, it is therefore of central importance to distinguish between those developments which promote the efficient international allocation of trade and capital flows and those which give rise to economic adjustments that run counter to efficient resource allocation. A satisfactory conceptual framework for making such a distinction must have at least two components. First, it must be able to identify the channels by which domestic policies and developments affect the balance of payments and exchange rates. Second, it must provide some basis for judging whether such effects, in given circumstances, are desirable or undesirable from an international standpoint.

## Factors Influencing Balance of Payments

The primary determinants of the current account of a country's balance of payments are (1) relative demand levels in the domestic economy and in its trading partners, and (2) relative competitiveness. This much is not controversial and provides a useful framework for analyzing balance of payments developments—though it has to be recognized that the relevant relationships cannot be established with a high degree of precision. The recent and prospective evolution of the trade and current accounts can be assessed with reference to past and anticipated developments in demand and competitiveness.[100] If forecasts are available for rates of domestic demand growth in the major countries over the relevant time horizon, estimates can be made of how the current account might evolve (other things held equal). Similarly, given an assumed evolution of domestic costs and prices and the pattern of exchange rates, estimates can be made of how these competitiveness factors will affect payments flows.[101] By adjusting the existing payments position for the estimated effects of lagged changes in exchange rates and of prospective changes in cyclical positions, it is thus possible to come to an assessment of the "underlying" balance of payments. The key indicators needed to make such an assessment are as follows: (1) a measure of economic activity (demand or output); (2) a measure of domestic inflation (costs or prices); and (3) a measure of the effective exchange rate.

The first two of these indicators can be projected on a country-by-country basis using standard forecasting techniques. The third (the exchange rate) can be easily observed ex post, but has proved difficult to project in any satisfactory manner. It is nevertheless of considerable interest to develop a framework for analyzing exchange rate developments and prospects, especially if judgments are required concerning whether a given pattern of exchange rates is to be regarded as sustainable or desirable. To do this, it is necessary to understand (and try to develop indicators for) the factors that underlie shifts in capital flows so as to provide a more comprehensive account of international economic interactions. This is a difficult exercise, in part because expectations (which are inherently hard to observe or model) play such an important role in determining the desire to acquire or dispose of external assets. A logical place to begin is by looking at the factors that influence the balance of domestic savings and investment (and therefore the net acquisition of foreign assets). These factors include developments in the fiscal position (which represents the net saving or dissaving of the public sector) as well as developments affecting the willingness of the private sector to save or invest. Indicators that may be useful in this context include: (1) a measure of the overall fiscal position; (2) gross private savings flows; (3) gross private investment; and (4) real interest rates.

---

[100] See "Issues in the Assessment of the Exchange Rates of Industrial Countries," International Monetary Fund Occasional Paper No. 29 (Washington: IMF, July 1984).

[101] The projections published by the Fund staff in its *World Economic Outlook* series are based on the working assumption that there will be no change in competitiveness from some base date. It is nevertheless of considerable importance to estimate how the lagged effects of changes in competitiveness that occurred prior to that date will affect balance of payments patterns.

## Criteria for Assessing Sustainability of Payments Balances

The calculation, as described above, of a set of "underlying current account balances" that is implied by existing policies and exchange rates can be a helpful focus in international surveillance. It can facilitate a dialogue aimed at assessing whether the projected trends can be considered sustainable or not.

A key issue in interpreting underlying payments balances is thus how to establish criteria for what should be considered sustainable. This is a particularly difficult analytical subject, on which it will undoubtedly be necessary to proceed gradually. A basis for approaching the issue is provided by the identity which equates the current account position (surplus or deficit) and the balance between domestic saving and investment. A sustainable current account position could therefore be defined as one in which the domestic savings and investment position of a country is sustainable, given the corresponding preferences of other countries, and the need to avoid an excessive buildup of external liabilities or assets.

The balance between domestic saving and investment can in turn be decomposed into the net financial balance of the public sector and the net financial balance of the private sector. The former is derived from the fiscal balance, which is an important indicator and policy tool in its own right. The latter is influenced by all the factors that affect private saving and investment decisions, including interest rates, the level and growth rate of real incomes, the return on physical capital, and demographic factors. The determinants of gross private saving and investment are subject to empirical estimation, although it has to be recognized that robust relationships are not always easy to establish.

The foregoing analysis suggests that the appraisal of policy interactions among industrial countries could be based on an analytical framework in which "underlying" current account positions (based on existing policies and exchange rates) would be compared with "sustainable" positions (derived from an assessment of the medium-run determinants of savings and investment). It is to be emphasized that international consistency of balance of payments positions is a necessary condition for their sustainability.[102]

It is clear that the prospective evolution of domestic variables is important in appraising both the underlying and the sustainable payments positions. Trends in GNP growth, domestic demand, and relative prices will affect movements in actual current account positions, while policies and developments that influence savings and investment propensities have an important bearing on the payments position that is sustainable over the longer term.

The foregoing implies that the setting and monitoring of objectives with respect to domestic variables is a matter of international concern, at least to some extent. The choice of whether a balance of payments disequilibrium should be corrected by exchange rate movement or a shift in relative rates of economic growth requires, for example, a view on the rate of growth in an individual country that should be considered attainable.

## Types of Economic Indicator: Uses, Scope, and Limitations

Indicators can be classified into three types: indicators of economic performance, which broadly speaking cover the more fundamental objectives of economic policy, that is, economic growth, employment, and balance of payments and price stability; indicators of economic policy, which cover variables over which the authorities have fairly close control, but which are not themselves components of economic welfare, that is monetary growth, exchange market intervention, the fiscal deficit, and so on; and indicators of intermediate variables, which are variables through which policies influence performance—savings and investment levels, interest rates, and exchange rates. Although the distinctions between these three different types of variable can sometimes be blurred, it is convenient to discuss them separately.

## Indicators of Economic Performance

*The balance of payments.* This variable can be considered either an objective of policy or an intermediate variable. For the major currencies with floating exchange rates, it is not an objective in the sense that these countries have quantified aims for the structure of their balance of payments. However, most countries would probably subscribe to the objective of restoring or maintaining a "sustainable" external payments structure, so as to limit the dangers of protectionist pressures and to minimize the costs and uncertainties that are involved when an unsustainable position emerges and has to be corrected. Moreover, from the point of view of surveillance, the restoration and maintenance of a balance of payments pattern that is adequately consistent with the domestic policies and

---

[102] This means that the "statistical discrepancy" in world balance payments statistics would have to be appropriately allowed for.

priorities of all members must be considered a key objective.

A widely used indicator related to the balance of payments is the current account surplus or deficit, and it seems appropriate that the current account balance remain the primary indicator of developments in the external sector.[103] As noted in the previous section, however, a satisfactory analytical framework for judging the sustainability of a given exchange rate pattern would involve an assessment of the "underlying," as well as the actual, current account position. This would involve making adjustments for the effects of recent exchange rate changes that had not yet been fully reflected in trade flows, for the impact on imports and exports of cyclical divergences from "normal" employment levels, and for any other special factors affecting payments flows in a given period.

Presentation of underlying balance of payments estimates would facilitate appraisal of the sustainability of the external positions implied by current policies and prospects. A sustainable balance of payments position can be defined as one in which the underlying current account surplus or deficit is matched by capital outflows or inflows that correspond to a country's desire to accumulate foreign assets or debts, and its capacity to service its external debt out of current foreign exchange earnings. For such a position to be internationally appropriate, it must also be compatible with the savings/investment preferences of other countries, and reasonably full employment of factors of production.

*Real output.* Perhaps the most widely used indicator of domestic economic performance is the rate of growth of GNP. As an indicator, GNP has the merit of comprehensiveness, widespread familiarity, and comparability across countries. Given the multiplicity of purposes for which it is employed, however, it should not be surprising that it is not equally suited for all purposes. As a measure of welfare, absorption per capita would be a better indicator, while as a measure of efficiency, output per unit of factor input might be superior.

The chief drawback of the GNP indicator for analyzing the international interaction of trends in output and demand, which is the natural focus of multilateral surveillance, is its level of aggregation. In particular, it is often desirable to distinguish the relative contribution of domestic and foreign sources of demand growth to any given change in overall GNP. So while GNP should remain the principal indicator of developments in the real economy, it needs to be supplemented with systematic presentation of developments and prospects in final domestic demand.

A more difficult issue than the choice of which indicator to use is the establishment of criteria by which objectives with respect to growth are to be judged, and performance assessed. Specifically, what rate of growth should be considered sustainable, given the constraints a country faces, its other objectives, and its obligations toward its trading partners? Such a calculation will involve, as a first step, estimating the underlying rate of growth of productive potential. This is not simple to estimate, since it depends not only on the rate of increase in available factors of production (the aggregate supply of labor and capital) but also on hard-to-observe variables such as the quality of factor inputs and the speed of technological progress. A second step would be to judge how large is the gap between existing and potential output levels and how quickly it is feasible to close such a gap. These are also difficult estimates to make, since they depend on factors such as the nature and extent of rigidities in goods and labor markets, the risk of igniting inflationary pressures, and the existence of other objectives (such as fiscal strengthening) that might legitimately constrain governments' freedom of maneuver. However, techniques for making judgments in these areas exist that enable the attainable rate of growth to be defined as the sum of (1) the growth in underlying capacity and (2) the rate of absorption of economic slack.

*Employment.* This indicator of economic performance is closely related to GNP growth. There are a variety of possible indicators in the employment field. The rate of increase in numbers employed is sometimes used as an indicator of "success in creating jobs." By this token, however, an economy with a rapidly growing population and labor force could appear to be more successful in the employment field than one with a slower growing population, even though the latter might have a lower rate of involuntary unemployment. A measure of labor market conditions that avoids this particular difficulty is the rate of unemployment, which is also in many respects a more visible objective for government policy. However, the rate of unemployment is itself not always an effective measure of involuntary unemployment. There may be categories of discouraged jobseekers (longer-term unemployed, young people remaining in education, women remaining in household work) not captured in published unemployment statistics.

As with GNP growth, a labor market indicator such

---

[103] The trade balance is another indicator of external developments that often attracts attention, particularly in the context of the need for trade liberalization and market access. The trade balance is also useful as a leading indicator of developments in the overall current account, since data related to trade are usually available on a more timely basis. In general, however, there seems little economic reason for drawing a distinction between trade in goods and trade in services.

as the unemployment rate needs a standard by which assessments can be made as to whether changes in the unemployment rate are satisfactory or not. A considerable literature exists on the "natural" rate of unemployment or the "nonaccelerating inflation rate of unemployment" (NAIRU). Although neither of these concepts is easy to apply in practice, they do provide a framework in which, for a given institutional setting, the existing unemployment rate can be judged too high (or, possibly, too low). A medium-term objective of policy would presumably be to move toward the NAIRU, and to do so at a pace that does not have seriously adverse consequences for other economic objectives, such as inflation control. It is also possible that governments may have medium-term objectives to reduce their NAIRU, say by structural measures that improve the flexibility of labor markets, and enable price stability to be maintained with a lower level of joblessness. To the extent that such structural goals can be quantified, it should be possible to factor them into medium-term employment objectives.

*Inflation.* This is another important indicator of economic performance. From a domestic standpoint, the key objective in most countries is probably to come as near as practically feasible to stability in consumer prices. Internationally, it may be more important to identify differentials in cost inflation (and where possible, reduce them), so as to facilitate the task of judging whether movements in nominal exchange rates are appropriate from the perspective of efficient adjustment. While costs and prices often move together, there can be differences in underlying trends. In an economy that has a more rapid rate of productivity increase in its manufacturing than in its service sector (as was the case, for example, in Japan in much of the postwar period), domestic price inflation could be higher than in its trading partners, while cost inflation in traded goods industries might be lower. This need not pose insuperable difficulties for the development and use of indicators, provided that the disparities are properly identified and allowed for.

Efficient adjustment also requires that any trend divergence in production costs in traded goods industries should be compatible with corresponding exchange rate trends. An inflation measure that has proved particularly useful in analysis is the rate of change of unit labor costs in those sectors of the economy that are most exposed to international competition. Being a measure of costs, it is more relevant to international competitiveness, and thus is better able to identify inflationary trends that have implications for balance of payments flows.

The foregoing discussion suggests that the inflation indicator that would be most useful in discussing external imbalances, exchange rate developments, and policy interactions is not necessarily the one that will be most familiar in a domestic economic context. Movements in the consumer price index contain adventitious elements that are only incidentally related to international competitiveness and underlying inflationary pressures. The GNP deflator is a superior indicator in many respects, although it still does not capture some important elements related to international competitiveness. A measure of labor costs per unit of output, perhaps normalized for differences among countries in cyclical position, would have important advantages. Its main drawbacks would be: (1) such an index is available only for the manufacturing sector of the economy; (2) the data from which it is compiled are produced with a lag; and (3) the concept is less familiar to policymakers. To some extent, however, it might be possible to reduce these shortcomings if it were decided to focus on such a measure as a central feature of surveillance.

## Indicators of Economic Policy

For expositional convenience, domestic macroeconomic policy can be divided into its monetary and fiscal aspects. In addition, countries that do not maintain either fully floating or rigidly fixed exchange rates have discretion in their management of reserves or exchange rate policies. Finally, the increased focus in recent years on structural policies suggests that it may be desirable to consider the possibilities of developing indicators in this field also.

*Monetary policy.* The most widely used indicator of monetary policy in the major industrial countries is the rate of growth of some monetary or credit aggregate. The specific aggregate that is used varies from country to country depending on the institutional characteristics of the country concerned and the robustness of empirical relationships.

Several issues arise in developing meaningful indicators for use in cross-country analysis. The first concerns whether the same measure of the money stock should be employed for all countries. On the one hand, it could be said that different definitions of monetary variables would inhibit comparability across countries. Some monetary authorities have selected a monetary target primarily on grounds of controllability; while others have preferred to target an aggregate that is closely linked with developments in the economy, even though the target itself cannot be closely controlled. Differences in criteria for the selection of monetary targets might cause difficulties when the monetary authorities were attempting to concert their policy stance—if, for example, they were trying to keep aggregate growth in the world money supply within some range, or to engage in offsetting policy responses to unwanted exchange rate developments.

Nevertheless, it would seem desirable to adapt the definition of monetary indicators to take account of conditions in particular countries. Generally speaking, when the authorities of a particular country have chosen a monetary aggregate for policy or monitoring purposes, this represents a careful choice based on analysis of the strength and stability of empirical relationships. It is likely to facilitate a meaningful dialogue, without undue loss of effective comparability, if the definitions used for purposes of international surveillance accord with those used for domestic policy formulation.

A second issue in the choice of monetary indicators concerns whether real or nominal variables should be used. It can be argued that it is the real money stock that determines the perceived liquidity of the private sector and therefore influences the willingness to spend. On the other hand, developments in the real money stock can be an ambiguous indicator. Under conditions of rising inflation, wealth-owners will seek to economize on real money balances and the real money stock will be observed to fall. Indeed, a systematic increase in the growth of the nominal money stock, causing an acceleration of inflation, will almost certainly lead to a decline in the real money stock. For this reason, and because the central goal of monetary policy is to keep inflation in check, it seems more appropriate to define monetary indicators (whether used as targets or as monitoring instruments) in nominal terms.

A third potential issue is how to handle unexpected shifts in the demand to hold money balances. If an upward shift in money demand can be identified, measured, and precisely offset by an equivalent adjustment in supply, it could be said that the stance of monetary policy has been kept unchanged. It would therefore be desirable to have an indicator that is adjusted for the effect of known shifts in the demand for money. The difficulty is, of course, that changes in demand are very hard to identify, particularly at the time they are occurring. One possibility would be to use interest rates as an indicator of a change in the balance between supply and demand in money and capital markets. But interest rates are also an ambiguous criterion, since an increase in interest rates may reflect a shift in the demand for money at given income levels, or an increase in credit caused by an incipient increase in nominal output. The implication of the foregoing is that the possible alternatives to the use of money growth rates as a primary indicator of the stance of policy all have drawbacks. A money stock indicator is still probably the best indicator of monetary policy in countries that use monetary targets, but it must be used with caution and in the light of surrounding developments.

Not all countries use monetary targets, of course. In countries with fixed exchange rates, the domestic money stock cannot be closely controlled by the authorities, since liquidity can enter or leave the country via overall balance of payments surpluses or deficits. Even in countries where there is greater freedom for exchange rate movement, monetary policy may be managed in the light of exchange rate and interest rate developments rather than to achieve target monetary objectives. For countries that do not have objectives for monetary aggregates, an alternative indicator of changes in monetary conditions will be necessary. One possibility, which would have the merit of facilitating international comparisons, would be to use interest rate differentials with major international currencies.

*Fiscal policy*. While the medium-term goal of monetary policy can be defined as the restoration and maintenance of an appropriate degree of price stability, the aims of fiscal policy are both macroeconomic and structural. At the macroeconomic level, governments have objectives for the budget deficit, related to the need for economic stabilization, as well as to a desire to limit the government's claims on the saving available for private investment. At the structural level, there may also be objectives for the structure and level of taxation and expenditure, with a view to enhancing incentives for efficient resource allocation, and limiting the absolute volume of real resources absorbed by the government.

In choosing how the macroeconomic objective relating to fiscal balance should be defined, a number of questions arise. These include: whether fiscal objectives should be established for the entire public sector, the general government, or for the central government alone; whether the objective should be for the actual fiscal deficit or for the "underlying" deficit (that is, whether the "policy-induced" fiscal change should be separated from the change attributable to purely cyclical factors); and whether or not the deficit that is monitored should be inflation corrected. Beyond these definitional issues, of course, lies the more fundamental question of what the fiscal objective should be, and whether independently determined objectives (such as zero deficits) are internationally consistent in terms of their impact on balance of payments flows.

The choice of whether the fiscal deficit that is measured should extend beyond the central government depends, to a considerable extent, on the scope of public sector activities that fall under the control of the fiscal authorities. Whichever level of government is selected as the primary focus for the fiscal indicator, however, it is important that the value of the indicator not be undermined by shifts in the classification of transactions (for example, from central to local government) that have substantial effects on the chosen indicator but little economic significance.

Concerning the choice of actual or cyclically corrected fiscal deficits, it is relevant to note that most governments express their aggregate fiscal objective in terms of some stated level for the actual fiscal deficit. This, indeed, is the indicator that most accurately measures the extent of the government sector's claims on financial markets. However, movements in the actual fiscal deficit can give a misleading impression of the thrust of fiscal policy when output is growing significantly faster or slower than its medium-term trend. In a phase of relatively rapid cyclical expansion, revenues tend to grow faster than expenditures and thus the budget deficit can shrink, even though policy-related fiscal measures may be tending to increase the deficit. Similarly, when the economy is stagnating, weak tax revenues may cause a budget deficit to widen even though the measures introduced by the authorities may in themselves be tending to strengthen the fiscal position. It seems desirable therefore to use indicators both of the actual and of the cyclically adjusted fiscal position.[104]

Adjustment for inflation poses some potentially more difficult issues. On the one hand, it can be argued that inflation effectively reduces the value of a government's outstanding debt with effects on wealth-holders that are similar to those of taxation. On the other hand, inflation adjustment can sometimes define away a real problem, as when the fiscal deficit itself is an important source of the pressures that give rise to inflation. In circumstances when inflation is low and stable, inflation adjustment is not needed to permit a meaningful comparison of fiscal conditions across countries or over time.

A more difficult issue than defining the fiscal deficit to be monitored is that of evolving criteria for assessing the appropriateness of countries' medium-term objectives in the fiscal field. While a country's objective for its fiscal deficit is intimately related to its domestic social and political priorities, it also has international implications. Changes in public sector saving or dissaving have consequences for the overall saving/investment balance in a country, and thus for its balance of payments situation. This is an area in which technical criteria are not easy to establish, and in which, therefore, it will be particularly useful to generate a multilateral dialogue.

*Exchange market policies.* Possible indicators in this area include the exchange rate and some measure of exchange market intervention. Since most of the major industrial countries pursue flexible exchange rate policies, the exchange rate itself is not regarded as a proximate instrument of policy. It is better viewed as an intermediate variable, and as such it is discussed further in the following section. Exchange market intervention, on the other hand, is a policy instrument that can be measured by the size of reserve movements over given intervals. It should be remembered, however, that exchange market intervention can sometimes take place in ways that do not affect reserves (for instance through borrowing and lending in foreign exchange by public sector entities). Moreover, the impact of intervention depends importantly on whether it is sterilized or nonsterilized. Concerning the criteria according to which exchange market intervention might be assessed, it seems reasonable to assume that reserve levels would, over time, tend to move toward some stable relation to external transactions (say, imports). For most major countries, it is unlikely that there would be any systematic ex ante intention to accumulate reserves, or run them down, in significant quantities. There would therefore be no prior standard (other than "no change") against which actual reserve movements would be compared. It would, however, be useful to compare intervention activities by one country with any offsetting activity on the part of trading partners; and to view exchange market intervention in the light of accompanying movements in exchange rates and interest rates.

*Structural policies.* Indicators of these policies are, by their nature, hard to devise. The structural policies that have been the focus of most attention in recent years have been those relating to deregulation, labor market rigidities, and trade restrictions. With regard to deregulation, it is possible to list the number of regulations eliminated or modified, and it is possible to provide analytical judgments about the effects of deregulation (in terms of reduced prices, for example, or an increased volume of transactions in the markets concerned). On the whole, it seems more practical to analyze the process of deregulation through ad hoc empirical studies, rather than through an attempt to devise specific and quantified indicators of objectives and performance. Labor market rigidities are thought to be manifested in a variety of ways, including inadequate flexibility of wages; wage levels that are too high; lack of geographical and occupational mobility; and inadequate training facilities. While many of these factors are not amenable to quantitative measurement through indicators, it does seem desir-

---

[104] For a review of the staff methodology for making cyclical adjustments to changes in the fiscal position, see "A Review of the Fiscal Impulse Measure," by Peter S. Heller, Richard D. Haas, and Ahsan S. Mansur, International Monetary Fund Occasional Paper No. 44 (Washington: IMF, May 1986).

able to use the indicator of unit labor costs described earlier to help in reaching judgments of whether developments in real wage rates are warranted by movements in labor productivity. As far as trade restrictions and protectionism are concerned, there is again no fully satisfactory way of developing quantitative indicators. There is thus little alternative to continuing to analyze the impact of trade restrictions in qualitative (albeit specific) terms, while to the extent possible including judgments of their quantitative significance.

## Indicators of Intermediate Variables

The channels by which policy variables affect the ultimate objectives of policy are not direct, nor are they fully predictable. For these reasons, it can be of value to develop indicators of those intermediate variables through which policy works to influence more fundamental objectives. Intermediate variables are not, in general, controlled directly by the policy authorities. However, they can be used to check whether the behavioral assumptions underlying the formulation of policy are an adequate representation of reality, and whether economic developments are following their anticipated path during the interval before measures have their effect on ultimate objectives. Intermediate variables can also be used to identify emerging problems of international consistency of policies.

*Interest rates and exchange rates.* An important channel by which policies influence ultimate economic objectives is through their effect on conditions in financial markets. In this connection, key roles are played by money and capital markets and the foreign exchange market. It is therefore of considerable interest to monitor developments in interest rates and exchange rates.

With regard to interest rates, a major determinant of individual saving and investment decisions is probably the level of the real interest rate. Notwithstanding the fact that inflationary expectations can only be measured indirectly, it nevertheless seems desirable to use some estimate of the real interest rate as the primary indicator for monitoring purposes. A helpful approximation in this connection, that is generally not seriously misleading, is to deduct from the nominal interest rate the rate of change in the GNP deflator over some recent period. While the level of real interest rates is of importance as an indicator of the incentive to save and invest, it is less significant than interest differentials in determining incentives to capital movements, and therefore exchange rate pressures. In monitoring real interest rates, it is therefore necessary to pay attention to international differentials in rates as well as to absolute levels.

As far as exchange rates are concerned, the indicator that is most relevant for purposes of international competitiveness and adjustment is the real effective exchange rate. This can be obtained by combining a measure of the nominal effective exchange rate (using currency weights derived from, say, the Fund's Multilateral Exchange Rate Model)[105] with a relative inflation estimate from the inflation indicator described above.

Since both interest rates and exchange rates are intermediate variables, it would be unrealistic to expect policy authorities to prescribe in advance any precise path for their expected evolution. Nevertheless, to the extent that the analysis of other indicators reveals underlying disequilibria in foreign exchange and capital markets, this analysis could signal the direction of possible changes in interest and exchange rates.

*Saving and investment balances.* As already implied, movements in interest rates and exchange rates are in turn influenced by underlying shifts in domestic saving and investment. Indeed, it is movements in interest and exchange rates that give causal content to the identity that makes the current account of the balance of payments equal to domestic savings minus domestic investment.

Any ex ante inconsistency at the global level between countries' balance of payments objectives or forecasts must be reflected in a similar global inconsistency between projected saving and investment trends. It may therefore be useful to keep track of actual or expected trends in savings and investment, in order to provide advance warning of possible inconsistencies. As noted earlier, the aggregate saving/investment balance of a country can be divided into the balance attributable to the public sector and that attributable to the private sector. The financial position of the public sector is, of course, the fiscal balance and has been discussed above. This can be complemented, for analytical purposes, with supplemental indices of saving and investment in the private sector.

## Concluding Observations

The preceding analysis has identified two sets of questions that need to be addressed in developing the use of indicators for surveillance purposes. A first set of issues concerns the analytical framework within which the analysis of indicators is to be set. A second concerns the nature of the indicators that are to be

---

[105] See Artus, J.R. and A.K. McGuirk, "A Revised Version of the Multilateral Exchange Rate Model," *Staff Papers*, International Monetary Fund (Washington), Vol. 28 (June 1981), pp. 275–309.

used. Beyond these issues, of course, lies the question of developing a framework of procedures that would enable the analysis of indicators to be used constructively as a tool of policy coordination.

*Analytical focus.* It has been argued that indicators should emphasize the international interactions of economic policies and performance, and should have regard to the medium-term framework in which policies are set. For these reasons, it would seem appropriate that the principal focus of analysis should be prospective balance of payments developments and their relationship with a sustainable position. This focus could be assisted by explicit consideration of the determination of domestic saving and investment balances.

*Nature of indicators to be used.* It has been argued that any variable that affects the level, distribution, or price of domestic output has implications for payments balances and exchange rates. Nevertheless, to be helpful in the surveillance process, indicators must be limited in number, quantifiable, timely, and relatively easy to interpret. In this connection, it is useful to distinguish among policy indicators, performance indicators, and intermediate variables. As policy indicators, the most relevant variables would seem to be the rate of growth of the monetary stock, the fiscal deficit ratio (on an actual and a cyclically adjusted basis), and changes in the level of gross reserves. Performance indicators would include the growth of domestic demand and GNP, the rate of change in the GNP deflator and in unit labor costs, and the current account of the balance of payments. Intermediate variables would be real interest and exchange rates, and the investment and saving ratios.

*Monitoring and procedures.* Procedural questions lie outside the scope of the present analysis. However, the practical implementation of an indicator-based analysis would appear to involve the following basic steps: (1) the development of a mechanism for collecting and analyzing national forecasts; (2) the establishment of procedures for discussing multilateral consistency of objectives and policies; and (3) "follow-up" procedures for discussion when developments diverge from what is desired or expected.

In conclusion, it should be noted that progress toward more systematic use of indicators will have to be gradual and evolutionary. This chapter has outlined one approach to the matter. However, it will undoubtedly be necessary to proceed cautiously, and to experiment with alternative forms of analysis in a search for the approach that provides the best basis for effective policy coordination.

# Appendix I
# Report of the Deputies of the Group of Ten: The Functioning of the International Monetary System

## Chapter I: Introduction

1. Following the invitation to Ministers of Finance recorded in the Declaration of the 1983 Williamsburg summit, the Ministers and Governors of the Group of Ten met in Washington on September 24, 1983 and had a preliminary exchange of views on the conditions necessary to improve the functioning of the international monetary system. They instructed their Deputies to met in the next few weeks "to identify the areas in which progressive improvements may be sought and to report to them at their next meeting to be held in early 1984."

2. In compliance with those instructions, in November 1983 the Deputies outlined a work program, subsequently approved by the Ministers and Governors, which identified the following four areas for investigation:
a) The functioning of floating exchange rates.
b) Strengthening multilateral surveillance.
c) Management of international liquidity.
d) The role of the International Monetary Fund (IMF).

3. In the organization of their work, the Deputies decided to undertake the elaboration of policy papers themselves, and to request the preparation of background studies to the international institutions represented in the Group—namely the IMF, the Organization for Economic Cooperation and Development (OECD), the Bank for International Settlements (BIS), and the Commission of the European Communities. The Deputies had the benefit of hearing the views of a senior representative of the International Bank for Reconstruction and Development (IBRD) at one of their meetings.

4. The Chairman of the Deputies presented a progress report on the Deputies' work to the Ministers and Governors at their Rome meeting on May 19, 1984. In the communique issued at the end of that meeting the Ministers and Governors "instructed their Deputies to continue their work, with a view to submitting a final report during the first half of 1985."

5. Following this Introduction, Chapters II, III, IV, and V deal in turn with the four subjects of the work program. They present an analytical overview of the issues and of the Deputies' discussions, including both the proposals on which a consensus was reached and those on which it was not. Chapter VI contains the Deputies' conclusions and their recommendations to the Ministers and Governors.

## Chapter II: The Functioning of Floating Exchange Rates

6. The Deputies have conducted a thorough examination of the working of the present system of floating exchange rates, taking stock of both the real experience acquired during the past decade and academic discussion. This chapter is devoted to a description and assessment of the system and to recommendations for improving its functioning, with a view to promoting greater exchange rate stability.

### General Considerations

7. The present exchange rate system came into being against a background of unsound domestic policies and divergent economic performances resulting in wide inflation differentials and large and persistent payments imbalances which rendered the previous par value system unsustainable. The sharp rise in oil prices and the widely differing policy responses exacerbated these problems and placed added strains on the international financial system. Following a transitional period, a more flexible exchange rate system was agreed upon in the 1976 meeting of the Interim Committee in Jamaica, which recommended changes in the Articles of Agreement permitting countries to choose their exchange rate regime while imposing on them certain general obligations (see Article IV).

8. Inflation, external disturbances, and divergent eco-

nomic performances continued to affect exchange market developments. The rapid expansion of international banking, the increasing sophistication and progressive deregulation of national financial markets, and the gradual removal of restrictions on capital flows have led to greater financial integration and capital mobility; while these developments may have contributed to short-term exchange rate movements, they have facilitated balance of payments financing and world economic growth.

9. Although most countries maintain some form of pegging, the main currencies all float separately or jointly against each other. These currencies are used to invoice and finance the bulk of world trade, are the basis for most of the Eurocurrency markets, and dominate foreign exchange trading. Over time, the system has evolved into a multicurrency reserve system in which the U.S. dollar is predominant while other main currencies have assumed secondary reserve roles. Since some three quarters of world trade and most invisible and capital transactions are conducted at floating rates, the present system can be described as a floating exchange rate system. In addition, regardless of their formal exchange rate arrangements, most countries have shown a greater willingness to let their exchange rates vary to prevent or to correct balance of payments disequilibria than under the par value system.

10. Since 1979 an arrangement which limits exchange rate fluctuations to narrow margins around agreed adjustable parities has been in operation within the context of the European Monetary System (EMS), involving a high degree of monetary cooperation and mutual surveillance. The arrangement is part of an effort to create an area of monetary stability and to achieve economic and monetary integration among countries closely linked by commercial flows as well as by institutional and political affinity.

11. The Deputies recognize that a country's choice of exchange rate regime is influenced by a number of factors, including the scale, composition, and direction of its trade as well as its openness to capital flows. Consequently, the degree of exchange rate stability deemed appropriate differs from country to country.

12. While countries have freedom in their choice of exchange rate arrangements, they must meet certain obligations in connection with their exchange rate policies. These obligations are set out in Section I of Article IV of the IMF Articles of Agreement, which reads as follows: "Recognizing that the essential purpose of the international monetary system is to provide a framework that facilitates the exchange of goods, services, and capital among countries, and that sustains sound economic growth, and that a principal objective is the continuing development of the orderly underlying conditions that are necessary for financial and economic stability, each member undertakes to collaborate with the Fund and other members to assure orderly exchange arrangements and to promote a stable system of exchange rates. In particular, each member shall:

**i)** endeavor to direct its economic and financial policies toward the objective of fostering orderly economic growth with reasonable price stability, with due regard to its circumstances;

**ii)** seek to promote stability by fostering orderly underlying economic and financial conditions and a monetary system that does not tend to produce erratic disruptions;

**iii)** avoid manipulating exchange rates or the international monetary system in order to prevent effective balance of payments adjustment or to gain an unfair competitive advantage over other members; and

**iv)** follow exchange policies compatible with the undertakings under this Section."

The Deputies reaffirm the overriding importance of these principles and policies and of ensuring their full implementation.

## Assessment of Floating Exchange Rates

13. It would be misleading to draw definite conclusions on the merits and demerits of the present system merely by comparing economic performance in the period of floating with that recorded under the par value system. Conditions during the floating rate period have been different in too many respects to allow such a comparison to be meaningful.

14. The Deputies agree that the existing exchange rate regime has shown valuable strengths. Exchange rate flexibility has made a positive contribution to external payments adjustment and to the maintenance of an open trade and payments system in a period of massive external shocks. It can help countries, especially the larger ones, to insulate their domestic price levels from inflation abroad, and can facilitate the pursuit of sound monetary policies geared more directly to domestic conditions. Furthermore, it is questionable whether any less flexible system would have survived the strains of the past decade, while attempting to preserve it would probably have led to increased reliance on restrictions on trade and capital flows.

15. The Deputies agree, however, that the functioning of the present system has also shown weaknesses. In particular the system has not adequately promoted sound and consistent policies. It has not prevented inadequate policies and divergent economic performances which have contributed to a high degree of short-term volatility of nominal exchange rates and to

large medium-term movements in real exchange rates.

**16.** The Deputies have noted that short-term exchange rate volatility has been substantial and has not shown any tendency to diminish over time. Although empirical studies conducted by the IMF have been unable to find a significant systematic link between short-term exchange rate volatility and the volume of international trade, concern has been expressed that volatility may discourage investment and trade by adding to uncertainty and to financial risks for investors and traders. However, foreign exchange markets appear to have developed effective hedging techniques available to most operators to reduce the risks associated with exchange rate volatility, generally at comparatively little cost.

**17.** Changes in real exchange rates are appropriate when they facilitate desirable adjustments by reflecting changes in underlying economic conditions and inducing corrections in policies. However, large movements in real exchange rates may lead to patterns of international transactions that are unlikely to be sustainable and that can pose difficult problems for domestic economies, involving a risk of protectionist pressures building up and resources being misallocated. If these exchange rate movements are subsequently reversed, a further disruption of trade and investment may result over the medium term.

**18.** The Deputies have noted that the influence on exchange rates of financial transactions not directly related to trade flows has steadily increased during the past decade. In turn, exchange rate variability may have contributed to greater capital movements. As a result, exchange rate determination has been increasingly influenced by conditions in capital markets, including relative interest rates and expectations regarding the impact of national policies and current and future economic performance.

**19.** The Deputies recognize that some variability is inherent in freely floating exchange rates. Since trade flows tend to adjust more slowly than financial flows, the impact of changes in current conditions is first reflected in financial and foreign exchange markets. Furthermore, in an uncertain environment the difficulty of assessing policy stances and underlying economic fundamentals may lead markets initially to overreact to unexpected developments. Finally, structural rigidities, including legal and regulatory constraints, may distort exchange rate relationships and retard adjustment.

**20.** While some events affecting exchange rates have been beyond the immediate control of national authorities, the Deputies are of the opinion that exchange rate instability has been fueled by inadequate and inconsistent policies that have led to divergent economic performance. Expectations in financial markets that inappropriate policies might not be quickly corrected have sometimes resulted in large exchange rate movements. Moreover, the perceived instability in current and future policy courses has made it difficult for market participants to find an anchor for exchange rate expectations.

**21.** While their study of the functioning of the exchange rate system has focused primarily on the objective of achieving greater stability among floating currencies, the Deputies are fully aware that attempts to maintain exchange rates at levels not in line with economic fundamentals and market forces can be very damaging, both to the countries concerned and to their trading partners. They have expressed their strong support for efforts regularly made by the IMF to persuade countries to adopt realistic exchange rate policies.

**22.** Given the high degree of interdependence and financial integration in the world economy, the Deputies recognize that no exchange rate system can provide full insulation from the effects of economic policies and performance in other countries. A stable international environment certainly requires sound and consistent policies that promote convergence of economic performance. But even if there were widespread and persistent application of non-inflationary policies, exchange rates and exchange rate expectations would be influenced by a number of factors, including the international configuration of fiscal policies, monetary policies, structural rigidities, domestic savings and investment patterns, and political uncertainties. More generally, different policy responses to exogenous disturbances can exert an impact on exchange rates.

## Proposals to Improve Exchange Rate Stability

**23.** The Group of Ten Ministers and Governors have already concluded that a return to a generalized system of fixed parities is unrealistic at the present time. In the view of the large majority of the Deputies, the adoption of alternatives to a system based on the floating of key currencies is unrealistic under current and foreseeable circumstances. All Deputies agree, however, that improvements are needed in the functioning of the present system.

**24.** While useful lessons can be drawn from the experience of the EMS as regards the promotion of policy convergence and exchange rate stability, the Deputies recognize that that system cannot be dissociated from the particular political and economic environment in which it operates and therefore cannot be readily extended to a broader and more heterogeneous context characterized by the presence of a plurality of reserve currencies. Such a system would run a much greater risk of being exposed to pressures similar to those which arose during the final phase of the par value system.

**25.** The Deputies agree that controls on international capital flows do not offer a desirable or effective means of achieving greater exchange rate stability. Their economic costs would be substantial. Given the close interrelationship between current and capital transactions, free capital movements are beneficial to the expansion of trade and to efficient resource allocation. Barriers to capital movements tend to hamper the smooth financing of current payments, distort market signals, and transfer more of the burden of external adjustment to exchange rates. Moreover, there is a constant danger of escalation and retaliation, with further negative consequences for trade growth and resource allocation.

**26.** The Deputies have also reviewed the role that official intervention in foreign exchange markets can play in reducing exchange rate volatility. They recognize that intervention has a role to play, if only a limited one, and in the light of recent experience they continue to endorse the conclusions reached on the basis of the Report of the Working Group on Intervention (see *Report of the Working Group on Exchange Market Intervention*, chaired by P. Jurgensen, January 1983), namely that:

**i)** intervention can be useful to counter disorderly market conditions and to reduce short-term volatility;
**ii)** intervention may also on occasion express an attitude toward exchange markets;
**iii)** intervention will normally be useful only when complementing and supporting other policies;
**iv)** countries should be willing to undertake coordinated intervention in instances when it is agreed that such intervention would be helpful.

**27.** Neither capital controls nor intervention can be relied upon to attain lasting stability of exchange rates. The Deputies have therefore focused on other means of achieving this goal through improved international cooperation.

**28.** The Deputies agree that the adoption of sound, credible, and stable policies in all countries, especially the major ones, can contribute fundamentally to exchange rate stability. Sound, non-inflationary macroeconomic policies contribute to greater convergence of economic performance among countries. Credible commitment to and persistent pursuit of such policies can also play an essential role in providing the foreign exchange markets with a firmer anchor for exchange rate expectations. Liberalization of capital markets and, more broadly, removal of restrictions and structural rigidities which hamper adjustment can reduce the burden placed on foreign exchange markets in absorbing short-term disturbances.

**29.** In view of the present high degree of economic interdependence, mutually consistent policies would also promote greater convergence of economic performance and thereby enhance exchange rate stability. Recognizing that the importance of external repercussions of national policies has often been underestimated, the Deputies agree that, in setting national policies, the international implications and interactions of those policies should receive an appropriately high priority.

**30.** In this connection, the Deputies have made a detailed review of the contribution that exchange rate developments might make to the evaluation of performance and policies. They note that these developments provide information on private markets' assessments of underlying economic conditions and of current and expected policies in the various countries. However, a wide range of factors beyond exchange rate developments should also be taken into account in assessing national policies and the need for consultation and policy discussion. These include, in addition to those mentioned in the IMF's principles for surveillance, developments and performance in the areas of fiscal policy (including the level of government expenditure), monetary policy, structural rigidities, and the openness of the economies to international trade flows.

**31.** Some Deputies made the proposal to introduce target zones for the exchange rates of major currencies because they believe that convergence of economic performance, while necessary, may not always be sufficient to achieve lasting exchange rate stability. They further believe that credible commitments to target zones would contribute to stabilizing market expectations and would promote greater international policy consistency by reinforcing multilateral surveillance. According to this proposal, the authorities concerned would define wide margins around an adjustable set of exchange rates devised to be consistent with a sustainable pattern of balances of payments. Target zones would be phased in progressively. They could, however, trigger consultations that would induce, step by step, more direct links between domestic policies and exchange rate considerations. This would not necessarily involve rigid commitments to intervene in exchange markets. Although the Deputies supporting this proposal recognize the difficulties of identifying equilibrium exchange rates, they believe these to be exaggerated, maintaining that arriving at a judgment about the appropriateness of the exchange rate of a currency is part of the current practices of the IMF. Some other Deputies recognize that there could be merits in this proposal and suggest that the technical aspects of a target zone approach should be further explored at an appropriate time.

32. Most Deputies, however, are of the view that reaching a consensus on the range of desirable exchange rates would prove extremely difficult. Given our imperfect knowledge of the determinants of exchange rate movements, the target zones would have to be too wide to serve as an anchor for expectations. Furthermore, even if agreement on an acceptable exchange rate pattern could be reached, there would still be the difficult task of allocating the burden of policy adjustment among the countries involved. Markets would inevitably test the zones, thereby adding to instability, and efforts to maintain exchange rates at levels incompatible with market sentiment could prove costly and ultimately unsuccessful. Above all, the constraints imposed on domestic policies by target zones might undermine efforts to pursue sound and stable policies in a medium-term framework. The majority of the Deputies, therefore, agree that the adoption of target zones is undesirable and in any case impractical in current circumstances.

33. All Deputies agree on the fundamental conclusion that greater exchange market stability requires close and continuing cooperation among countries and a strengthening of international surveillance to improve the compatibility of policies among countries and the convergence of economic performance around sustainable, non-inflationary growth.

## Chapter III: Strengthening International Surveillance

### General Considerations

34. The IMF plays a central role in surveillance. As mentioned earlier (paragraph 12), the IMF Articles of Agreement contain important obligations regarding members' policies. They also include specific principles and procedures for the conduct of international surveillance to assure that these obligations are fulfilled (Article IV, Section 3 and Executive Board Decision No. 5392-(77/63)).

35. Surveillance functions are also performed by other institutions and consultative groups which operate under different legal frameworks and procedures. The Deputies have noted in particular the functions performed by the OECD, the BIS, the General Agreement on Tariffs and Trade (GATT), the IBRD, and the European Communities, and by various international ministerial groups. The Deputies have concentrated their attention on IMF surveillance, with a view to improving its effectiveness and consistency with surveillance in other forums.

36. The Deputies agree that no major changes are required in the present institutional setting for exercising surveillance over national policies. Nevertheless, they agree that during the period of floating exchange rates surveillance has not been as effective as desirable in influencing national policies and in promoting underlying economic and financial conditions conducive to exchange rate stability. Surveillance has not been sufficiently effective in inducing policy changes in countries which have adequate access to external financing and do not require an IMF-supported adjustment program. These countries appear to have been able on occasion to sustain policy courses not fully compatible with the goals of international adjustment and financial stability. A number of improvements, therefore, are needed in order to make the process more effective.

37. The Deputies recognize that in the implementation of surveillance the focus has tended to be on a country-specific approach, with less attention being given to the interaction of national policies and economic structures. The effectiveness of surveillance has also been weakened in certain instances by lack of mutual understanding of the impact of particular policies and of an agreed analytical framework, which have sometimes made international consensus on the appropriateness of policies more difficult to achieve.

### Proposals to Strengthen Surveillance

38. The Deputies reaffirm that effective surveillance presupposes full cooperation by every country. Countries must therefore be ready to recognize the international implications of their policies and to give them more weight in their decision-making process. Surveillance, however, is a delicate matter, since it impinges on the conduct of national policies. The Deputies emphasize that strengthened surveillance requires enhanced dialogue and persuasion through peer pressure, rather than mechanically imposed external constraints. All Deputies believe that mutually agreed procedures would be helpful, but some Deputies think that an element of constraint will also be required if surveillance is to be made more effective. While stressing that the sensitivity of the issues involved in surveillance necessitates preserving confidentiality, some Deputies suggest that greater publicity for policy conclusions could be an instrument to further the adoption of appropriate policies.

39. The Deputies stress the need for symmetry and evenhandedness in the exercise of surveillance. Countries should be treated in the same manner irrespective of their size, exchange rate regime, or financial position. However, equal treatment cannot mean uniformity of prescriptions. Policy advice must take account

not only of different situations, economic structures, and institutional settings but also of the impact of individual countries on the world economy.

40. The Deputies emphasize that to be effective surveillance over exchange rates must concern itself with the assessment of all the policies that affect trade, capital movements, external adjustment, and the effective functioning of the international monetary system. Such an assessment should cover not only macroeconomic policies but also the micro policies and structural features that could weaken performance and induce exchange rate instability. It should also include a more explicit analysis of domestic policies in the context of the world economy, so that interdependences and mutual repercussions are fully brought out and taken into account.

41. While the present institutional framework for surveillance is considered adequate, the Deputies agree that the existing channels need to be used more effectively and coordinated better. They also agree that the central role of the IMF in surveillance should be preserved. At the same time, they underline that other institutions, consultative bodies, and groups of more limited membership should continue to play their role in the surveillance process. In this regard, they have noted the important role played by the OECD in the surveillance of the economic policies of the industrial countries.

42. In considering ways of strengthening surveillance, a distinction has been made between surveillance in the form of country-specific consultations with an international institution (e.g., bilateral surveillance), and surveillance which focuses on the international adjustment process and the interaction of national policies (e.g., multilateral surveillance). The Deputies' detailed proposals are grouped below under the headings of "Article IV Surveillance" and "Multilateral Surveillance."

## Article IV Surveillance

43. The Deputies agree that Article IV consultations should continue to be primarily concerned with the broad range of macroeconomic policies, including exchange rate policies, bearing on a country's external position and on international adjustment. Within this overall framework, they propose that consultations should also give more emphasis to analysis of capital account development; government policies which hinder the efficient operation of exchange and capital markets; and, more generally, impediments to the international adjustment mechanism caused by trade restrictions and other protectionist measures, such as policies to provide special incentives to exports or discourage imports, other market-distorting policies, and structural rigidities. In order to achieve greater consistency and continuity of action, policy analyses and recommendations should be viewed in a medium-term framework.

44. The assessment of the current state of individual countries and the world economy and the formulation of policy recommendations would be facilitated by better data and stronger analytical foundations. The Deputies are of the view that IMF surveillance activities can play a major role in improving the information on and analysis of individual economies. In this connection they put forward the following suggestions:
(i) consultation reports should be used to identify necessary improvements in the scope, quality, and timeliness of data provided to the IMF by national authorities; (ii) the empirical and analytical basis of policy judgments should be made as explicit as possible, whether by the IMF or by member governments; (iii) techniques for analyzing medium-term external debt and debt-servicing scenarios should be improved as part of the ongoing work to strengthen surveillance over external indebtedness. Where appropriate, closer cooperation with the IBRD in all these areas should be sought.

45. The Deputies agree that, in order to ensure that consultation conclusions have greater influence, the IMF should provide more candid assessments of national policies and their domestic and international impact as well as precise suggestions for policy changes. Differences of views between the IMF and national authorities should be spelled out and discussed. For industrial and developing countries whose policies and performance are of greatest concern for the world economy, a confidential exchange of views between the Managing Director and the Finance Minister should be envisaged at the end of the consultation process. In addition, to ensure an adequate follow-up to the consultation conclusions, countries should be requested to present a report outlining the measures introduced or considered to deal with the problems identified by the IMF and to respond to specific policy suggestions. The degree of implementation and effects of policy recommendations should in all cases be reviewed in ensuing consultations and consultation reports.

46. The Deputies consider that it could be helpful if the IMF made greater use of the supplemental surveillance procedures in the face of exchange rate and other developments that may be important or may have important effects on other members, or that have implications for the operation of the international monetary system; to this end they invite the IMF to review the arrangements set up in 1977 and 1979 for invoking these procedures.

47. The Deputies note that the IMF has played an essential role as coordinator of multilateral efforts to respond to external debt problems. In most cases this role has involved the development of adjustment programs supported by use of IMF resources, but recently some debtor countries have been working with the IMF and their major creditors to explore the possibility of "enhanced" surveillance with the aim of facilitating non-IMF financing in connection with multiyear debt reschedulings. The Deputies encourage the IMF to continue to develop such procedures on a case-by-case basis, reflecting general understandings that would be adopted by the Executive Board. Similar procedures might be considered for countries whose limited access to external finance could be improved with IMF assistance and advice.

48. The Deputies agree that the basic confidentiality of the exchange of information and discussions between the IMF and its members should be preserved. The view has been expressed, however, that giving some publicity to consultation conclusions could help make them more influential. In particular, it has been suggested that a public statement might be made by the Managing Director, on his own authority and without Executive Board approval, at the end of the consultation process; the statement, which could be based on his own summing-up of the Executive Board discussion, would give a brief assessment of a country's policies and prospects and would indicate the broad direction of suggested policy changes. It has also been suggested that the Executive Board consider authorizing the release of consultation documents, in whole or in part, at the request of the member country concerned.

## Multilateral Surveillance

49. The Deputies agree that multilateral surveillance should be strengthened. It should concentrate on countries which have a large impact on the world economy. Effective multilateral surveillance may require a reinforcement of existing procedures as well as consideration of the introduction of new arrangements.

50. The specific content of multilateral surveillance should be the examination of the external repercussions of national policies and their interaction in the determination of the global environment. The Deputies agree that the approach to these issues should be mainly judgmental in nature. In this respect, the regular monitoring of key economic developments can help to assess the consistency and mutual compatibility of national policies in the light of the objectives of international adjustment and financial stability, and hence to identify situations that warrant policy reviews and consultations. Special attention should be devoted to developments in exchange rates, trade, and capital flows, which are the principal elements of international interaction, as well as to the broad range of economic policies underlying them.

51. The Deputies propose that the IMF should periodically prepare documents analyzing the international repercussions of national policies of Group of Ten countries and of their interaction in the determination of exchange rate developments and international adjustment. More specifically, they consider it appropriate that the World Economic Outlook (WEO) paper should devote a separate chapter to these issues, setting out the principal quantitative aspects and providing an analytical framework for policy discussions.

52. The Deputies propose that the Group of Ten Ministers and Governors should review the main conclusions emerging from the chapter of the WEO on the international repercussions and interaction of their policies, as appropriate. Some Deputies propose that the conclusions of these reviews should be summarized in the form of a statement by the Chairman, containing the views of the Group on the appropriateness of its members' policies.

53. The Deputies agree that Working Party No. 3 of the OECD should continue its regular review of major countries' fiscal and monetary policies and the way these interact internationally, with particular reference to the evolution of external positions and exchange rates. While these interactions are in many respects of a short-term nature, it has become increasing appropriate for the Working Party's deliberations to have a medium-term perspective, and to pay greater attention to structural features, such as rigidities in goods, labor, and financial markets, that have a bearing on the international adjustment process. In the latter connection, it is to be welcomed that the annual examinations of national economies in the Economic and Development Review Committee of the OECD now cover selected structural issues in depth.

54. The key role in fostering trade liberalization and the removal of barriers which restrict or hamper free trade pertains to the GATT. The Deputies believe that the GATT should have broad powers to exercise surveillance over all forms of trade restriction including bilateral restraint agreements and other national trade-restricting practices and policies. Close cooperation between the IMF and the GATT should be maintained. The IMF should place emphasis in its policy analyses and recommendations, whether within a bilateral or a multilateral framework, on the removal of trade-restricting practices and on the implementation of GATT recommendations and policies.

## Chapter IV: The Management of International Liquidity

55. The Deputies have in the main confined their discussions to two aspects of the management of international liquidity. The first and more general issue related to the changes in the international financial system since the transition to floating exchange rates, and the implications of these changes for the creation and distribution of international liquidity. The second and more specific issue was the present and future role of the SDR in the international monetary system.

## General Considerations

56. Under the gold-exchange standard, international liquidity was virtually equated with monetary authorities' holdings of reserve assets, comprising gold, foreign currencies, and reserve claims on the IMF. Reserves were generally "owned," since international liquidity acquired through credit arrangements played only a minor role. The demand for reserves was generally seen as a fairly stable and predictable function of the value of world trade and payments imbalances.

57. The ending of the obligation to defend fixed exchange rates has substantially changed the rationale for holding international reserves. It does not appear, however, to have led to any appreciable decline in the overall demand for reserves. There appear to be several reasons for this. Most floating countries have continued to intervene in foreign exchange markets to varying extents. Other countries have also continued to manage their exchange rate or to peg it [their currency] to another currency or to a currency basket. Thus reserve balances have been maintained for intervention purposes. In addition, many countries have held precautionary reserve balances in an attempt to protect themselves from the uncertainties arising from larger payments disequilibria and exchange rate fluctuations. Finally, reserves have been acquired as a means of demonstrating creditworthiness and preserving access to financial markets.

58. On the supply side, the international credit markets have provided new channels for meeting the rapid growth in external financing requirements and the demand for reserves quickly and efficiently. However, those countries that do not have access to international capital markets or that have lost creditworthiness have continued to rely primarily on official channels and conditional credit to finance current account imbalances and acquire reserves.

59. As a result of these changes, international liquidity has come to embrace not only monetary authorities' actual holdings of reserve assets but also credit arrangements which permit the acquisition of reserves from private and official sources. Thus, the adequacy of international liquidity can no longer be assessed primarily on the basis of recorded reserve holdings, but must also take account of countries' creditworthiness and the availability of official sources of financing.

60. Countries can obtain reserves from financial markets provided they maintain their creditworthiness, which is mainly a function of their own domestic policies and performance. However, conditions in international markets are affected by the financial policies of reserve-currency countries. Therefore, the terms on which reserves are supplied by the markets are likely to reflect not only the borrowers' own policies and performance but also those of the major industrial countries.

61. The preponderance of market-supplied international liquidity has reduced the scope for influencing the process of reserve creation directly. Only a small share of total liquidity, arising from IMF-related reserve assets and credit provided under bilateral and multilateral official credit arrangement, is amenable to some form of direct control. These developments have increased the importance of pursuing sound domestic policies in order to safeguard creditworthiness. The strictness of the resulting discipline inevitably varies with countries' economic structures and states of development.

62. As a result of the evolution of the international monetary system in the post-Bretton Woods era, financial markets have thus acquired a crucial role in the provision of liquidity in the world economy. In the process, the concept of international liquidity has widened and become more complex, and the smooth functioning of the system has come to depend more on countries' national policies and creditworthiness and on the working of market mechanisms.

63. The Deputies agree that, while the process of liquidity creation has been made more flexible and the scope for countries to manage their international reserve position has generally increased, the working of the system has not been entirely satisfactory. The strong inflationary pressures of the seventies and the major external debt problems of the eighties suggest that during most of this period the supply of international liquidity has been ample, if not excessive. Instances of sharp contraction in the availability of international credit have also occurred. In the view of some of the Deputies this suggests that present arrangements for the provision of liquidity have not been optimal and that, while ultimately producing very powerful effects, they have not always been conducive to a gradual adjustment toward steady non-inflationary growth of the world economy. They believe that sudden and marked shifts in the terms and conditions on which

international liquidity has been made available, late recognition of and abrupt response to changes in creditworthiness, and the very limited access certain groups of countries have to market borrowing, are factors that cannot be ignored. Other Deputies emphasize that sharp shifts in liquidity have generally reflected inadequate underlying policies that the stability of the system depends primarily on all countries pursuing sound policies to achieve sustainable non-inflationary growth.

## Proposals Concerning International Liquidity

**64.** The Deputies agree that improvements in the provision of international liquidity need not be sought through fundamental changes in the system. They also recognize that for the foreseeable future financial markets must be expected to continue to supply the bulk of international liquidity and that official channels will have a significant supplementary role. The Deputies have considered a number of measures designed to strengthen the working of the system by enhancing the efficiency of market processes and by fostering the pursuit of appropriate policies in all countries. The Deputies have also considered various proposals relating to the IMF's ability to meet systemic liquidity needs.

**65.** Three sets of measures have been proposed by the Deputies in order to improve the operation of financial markets in the provision of international liquidity. First, international institutions should be encouraged to continue to improve the collection and dissemination of all the data relevant to the markets' assessment of individual countries' creditworthiness, and banks should seek to improve their methods of risk evaluation. Second, countries should press forward steadily with the deregulation of capital markets and the liberalization of capital movements. Third, monetary authorities should continue to place emphasis on strengthening the supervision of banks operating in the international markets, especially with a view to establishing adequate capital requirements, applying consolidated balance-sheet reporting, and encouraging greater convergence of regulatory practices. The BIS has an important role to play in this respect. The Deputies stress that in monitoring international banking activities, the authorities should pay due regard to possible macroeconomic consequences of prudential measures.

**66.** The Deputies emphasize that a smooth provision of liquidity through financial markets is possible only in an environment of sound, non-inflationary policies in all countries. An appropriate evolution of international liquidity also depends on the willingness of countries to take account of the international implications of their domestic policies. The Deputies therefore agree that multilateral surveillance has a key function to play in this area as well, to foster policies consistent with a more stable evolution of international liquidity. Indeed, the IMF Articles of Agreement call on members to collaborate with the IMF and with other members in pursuit of the objective of "better international surveillance of international liquidity" (Article VIII, Section 7). In particular, surveillance should guide countries in their choice between financing and adjustment of external payments imbalances; facilitate the maintenance or, where necessary, the restoration of creditworthiness; and foster closer cooperation among countries whose policies exert an important influence on conditions in world financial markets.

**67.** The above considerations indicate that surveillance of exchange rate policies and surveillance of international liquidity cover a great deal of common ground. The Deputies therefore stress the need for their implementation to be closely integrated.

**68.** The Deputies are aware that some countries have not had significant access to international financial markets and are therefore largely dependent on other sources of financing for the acquisition of reserves until they can restore or gain creditworthiness. They recognize that the provision of concessional financing is necessary for many of these countries, and that officially supported financing can help maintain and strengthen their external positions. The Deputies therefore suggest that these countries be provided official financing on appropriate terms in support of sound policies which can help promote creditworthiness.

## Present and Future Role of the SDR

**69.** The First Amendment of the Articles of Agreement enabled the IMF to allocate SDRs "to meet the need, as and when it arises, for a supplement to existing reserve assets" (Article XV, Section 1 [of the Articles currently in force]). The main purpose of creating the SDR was to make the supply of reserves less dependent on the official settlements balance of the United States and to provide an instrument to counteract reserve shortages. Moreover, by offering non-reserve countries the possibility of acquiring reserves without having to obtain balance of payments surpluses, the SDR could alleviate somewhat the asymmetry of external constraints on national policies. The Second Amendment of the Articles of Agreement called on members to collaborate, with the objective of "making the special drawing right the principal reserve asset in the international monetary system" (Article VIII, Section 7).

**70.** Despite the objectives stated in the Articles, the SDR has not assumed a major role in the system, its share in total foreign exchange reserves having actually declined during the last decade. The use of the SDR as a unit of account in private transactions remains limited and the market for SDR-denominated assets and liabilities, after an initial spurt, has not shown any tendency to develop further.

**71.** The limited success of the SDR as an international reserve asset can be attributed in part to its features and restricted usability. Developments in the monetary system have also lessened official interest in an internationally issued and administered reserve asset. The expansion of international financial markets has provided a flexible and efficient source of reserves for many countries, and the emerging multicurrency reserve system has reduced dependence on a single currency in international settlements and reserve holdings.

**72.** The Deputies recognize that these developments have affected the rationale for the SDR, including the objective of placing the SDR at the center of the system as the main reserve asset. Nevertheless, the Deputies, noting the SDR's owned-reserve nature, believe that the instrument may still have a useful role to play in meeting the long-term global need for supplementing reserves in a system largely based on borrowed reserves. In this context, the Deputies have considered various ways of making the SDR available as a safety net for future contingencies, including the possibility of private markets being unable to respond adequately to a legitimate long-term global need for international liquidity. They have not agreed, however, that any of these approaches would be desirable or appropriate at this stage.

**73.** The Deputies have not reached a consensus on the question of whether the present situation calls for new allocations of SDRs. A number of Deputies consider that there is at present no clear evidence of a long-term global need to supplement international reserves, given the present state of total reserves and lending from international markets. Other Deputies, however, favor resumption of SDR allocations on the basis of the arguments described below.

**74.** According to some of the Deputies, severe strains in liquidity conditions have built up in the system and are reflected in the decline of reserves in relation to imports and foreign debt, the lopsided distribution of reserves, and the rise of barter trade. While an SDR allocation on a reasonable scale would not eliminate these strains entirely, these Deputies would see it as a means of assisting countries in their search for international liquidity and of facilitating the international adjustment process. Other Deputies, however, have expressed reservations about this analysis. In their view, the difficulties encountered by a number of countries are primarily an indication of their lack of creditworthiness and are not related to a general shortage of liquidity. Even in the recent period of debt problems, reserves have increased significantly, particularly for non-oil developing countries in aggregate. Moreover, the decline in reserves which occurred in 1981–82 followed a period of excessive inflation and rapid reserve gains. These Deputies stress that SDR allocations are not the appropriate tool for providing finance to countries whose access to international credit markets has been jeopardized and suggest that they might result in delaying necessary adjustment. Furthermore, even a substantial allocation would provide no more than a minimal benefit to debtor nations' reserves.

**75.** Some Deputies have proposed that existing rules governing the conditions, the amount, and the distribution of allocations should be supplemented by an arrangement whereby SDRs would be used to finance IMF adjustment programs. To this end, participants in the SDR Department would place all or part of their allocations at the disposal of the IMF. These SDRs could then be channeled to countries in need of reserves in support of appropriate adjustment programs. This proposal has been criticized on various grounds. Some Deputies doubted whether the allocation of SDRs for these purposes would be consistent with the Articles of Agreement. The proposal could also blur the distinction between the SDR and conditional IMF credit, and the lending or transfer of SDR allocations to the IMF could raise legislative difficulties within countries. Finally, the use of SDRs to expand the IMF's resources for conditional lending is viewed by these Deputies as unnecessary, since the IMF has adequate resources to fulfill its responsibilities for the foreseeable future.

**76.** In view of some of the Deputies, quite apart from short-term considerations relating to the state of liquidity, a resumption of SDR allocations is justified by longer-term, systemic considerations. These Deputies point to the fact that the long-term growth of trade must be supported by an expansion of international reserves, and that an increased share of the SDR in official reserves would increase the stability of the system. These Deputies advocate that SDRs should be injected into the system in accordance with a steady quantitative rule so designed that their relative weight in official reserves would expand gradually over time without endangering discipline. Other Deputies, however, believe that international financial markets and official channels provide adequate means of meeting the global demand for reserves, and are concerned that regular SDR allocations would result in unnecessary and excessive liquidity creation.

**77.** A further proposal examined by the Deputies is the establishment of an SDR-based IMF. Under this scheme, which would involve merging the General Department and the SDR Department, IMF lending would result in the creation of SDRs and reimbursement in their cancellation. In the view of its proponents this proposal, while not entailing any basic change in members' rights and obligations, would equalize the characteristics of claims on the IMF, streamline the IMF's operations, and render them more neutral with respect to exchange rates and monetary aggregates. Moreover, quota increases under the proposed scheme would not entail the provision of national currencies, thus obviating the need for national budgetary appropriations. Most Deputies consider this proposal too far-reaching and not realizable at the present time. In their view, such a major change would not enhance the IMF's ability to fulfill its responsibilities and could undermine its mutual assistance character. Moreover, the abolition of subscription payments in convertible currencies could jeopardize confidence in the institution.

**78.** In conclusion, the Deputies have not reached agreement on any of the specific proposals described above. However, they recognize that the SDR may still have a useful role in meeting the long-term global need for reserves and in this context in providing a safety net for future contingencies. In these circumstances, the Deputies support the intention of the IMF Executive Directors to carry out a comprehensive review of the future role of the SDR in the system.

## Chapter V: The Role of the IMF

**79.** The IMF plays a key role in the international monetary system. It oversees and guides the operation and the evolution of the system, providing a legal framework for consultation and cooperation. It promotes the adoption of domestic policies consistent with balance of payments adjustment and financial stability, the maintenance of a trade and payments system free from restrictions, and exchange rate stability. It supplements the stock of official reserves through SDR allocations and its credit activity, which results in the creation of reserve positions. The main instruments available to the IMF to further its objectives are the exercise of surveillance over countries' policies, the extension of financial assistance conditional on the adoption of adjustment policies, and the authority to allocate SDRs. The IMF's surveillance functions have been examined in Chapter III of this Report, and issues concerning the SDR in Chapter IV.

This chapter concentrates on the functions of the IMF in providing temporary balance of payments assistance and promoting adjustment.

## General Considerations

**80.** The policies governing the use of IMF resources, embodied in the Articles of Agreement (notably Article V) and in Executive Board Decisions, stipulate that IMF financing is to be provided (i) on a temporary basis; (ii) in amounts related to members' quotas; (iii) conditionally upon the adoption of policies to correct payments problems over the short-to-medium term. These policies are designed to ensure that the revolving nature of IMF resources is preserved and that claims on the IMF can be mobilized quickly in cases of balance of payments need. The Deputies wish to stress that IMF resources through the years have been used and provided by all categories of members, a factor which has reinforced the universal character of the institution and helped maintain the broad support of its membership.

**81.** An unprecedented conjunction of large and persistent external imbalances in many countries over the last 12 years has led the IMF to expand considerably its financial assistance in support of external adjustment programs. Lending policies have been modified, leading to a lengthening of program periods and to the introduction of a temporary policy of enlarged access which allows members to obtain credit up to a multiple of quotas in support of comprehensive adjustment programs. As a result the IMF has borrowed substantially from official sources to supplement its quota resources. In addition, the IMF has come to play a role as a catalyst and coordinator of external finance from other sources for countries facing severe problems in servicing their external debt. The Deputies note that in recent years requests for IMF credit and assistance have come almost entirely from developing countries.

**82.** The Deputies consider that the IMF has responded flexibly and effectively in the face of disturbances which were threatening world financial stability and that its adjustment programs have been most valuable in the process of restoring confidence and viable external positions. They encourage the IMF to continue its efforts in this area. They stress, however, that as more normal payments and creditworthiness situations in debtor countries return, the IMF should revert to its traditional role.

**83.** The Deputies recognize that the IMF has managed its operations prudently and that its liquidity position is currently strong. Nonetheless, they are concerned that, if they persist, the lengthening of program and repayment periods and the prolonged use of IMF resources may adversely affect the revolving nature of its financing and the liquidity of members' claims on the IMF. This in turn would weaken the IMF's ability to grant financial assistance and members' willingness to provide resources.

84. The Deputies recognize that the correction of payments imbalances requires complementary measures in the areas of demand management and structural adjustment, including realistic exchange rates. However, they are concerned that in some cases countries with balance of payments difficulties have not adopted adequate adjustment policies early enough, or have adopted programs that were not sufficiently rigorous and comprehensive. This has been a factor in the lengthening of adjustment periods and the more extended use of IMF credit, and hence in the requests for the injection of additional resources. Recourse to frequent increases in resources, including borrowing, on the one side, and less effective adjustment on the other, tend to confuse the IMF's functions with those of a development finance institution.

## Strengthening the Role of the IMF

85. The Deputies emphasize the importance of preserving the monetary character of the institution and the revolving nature of its resources. The ability of the IMF to continue to play its role in promoting adjustment and providing conditional financing when the need arises depends on these fundamental features being preserved. In turn this requires that four conditions be met: (i) that the IMF be able to command adequate resources; (ii) that it normally finances its lending from quota resources; (iii) that the conditionality in IMF programs continues to place emphasis on the need to restore a sustainable balance of payments and external debt position in the short-to-medium term; (iv) that the universal character of the IMF be maintained.

86. The Deputies reiterate that quotas should represent the basic source of IMF financing and that recourse to borrowing to supplement these resources should be made only in exceptional circumstances. They recognize, in this connection, that the ability of the IMF to perform its functions effectively depends on the adequacy of its resources relative to the legitimate needs of its members. While the bulk of balance of payments financing should continue to be met through other private and official sources, IMF credit should be available on a sufficient scale to provide meaningful support to members and to serve as an important catalyst for other lending by providing confidence that the borrower is pursuing sound policies.

87. The IMF's resources are intended to deal both with balance of payments financing needs that arise in normal conditions and with exceptional situations involving a threat to the stability of the system. The Deputies agree that, barring unforeseen circumstances, the recent increase in IMF quotas and the enlargement and expansion of the GAB [General Arrangements to Borrow] provide the IMF with an adequate basis to fulfill its responsibilities over the next few years. However, they recognize that negotiations on quotas and borrowing arrangements are complex and time consuming. They therefore suggest that the IMF undertake a study of alternative techniques that would provide resources to deal with exceptional circumstances without involving an immediate increase in members' subscriptions, thus adding to the operational flexibility of the IMF.

88. The Deputies consider that the IMF should continue to implement the policies on the use of its resources in a prudent manner, and that a return to normal access policies is desirable. In this respect, they reaffirm that the policy of enlarged access is temporary, should continue to be phased down, and should be terminated as soon as the situation of external payments permits.

89. The Deputies reiterate the importance of effective conditionality in the implementation of IMF programs. They stress the need for high-quality and sufficiently comprehensive adjustment programs, including measures tackling structural problems, to be undertaken promptly in order to allow balance of payments difficulties to be dealt with quickly and effectively. The Deputies also see a need for a systematic examination by the IMF of the issues of prolonged use of its resources by some members and of the arrears it is owed. They consider that steps should be taken to deal with these problems.

## IMF/IBRD Cooperation

90. The Deputies note that, while the IMF and the IBRD share certain broad objectives and while their activities are closely interconnected, their functions differ. The Bank's responsibilities relate primarily to the provision of long-term finance to developing countries and the promotion of development, while those of the IMF are concerned with exchange stability, international payments, and balance of payments adjustment of industrial and developing countries. In the case of developing countries these functions are complementary, since macroeconomic balance is a precondition for growth and development, and over the longer run, project and sectoral efficiency and realistic investment priorities can be crucial to sustained bal-

ance of payments adjustment. Coordination between the two institutions is therefore essential to ensure the effective achievement of their common objectives, but it needs to be based on their separate responsibilities for implementing the several tasks entrusted to each.

91. The Deputies agree that there is considerable scope for closer cooperation between the two institutions. The main purpose of such cooperation should be to ensure that their financing programs provide a comprehensive and mutually supporting approach to countries' adjustment problems and that they provide consistent policy advice. This would increase the effectiveness of both institutions and enhance the prospects for increasing private investment flows to developing countries.

92. The Deputies emphasize that the two institutions have different mandates, functions, financial structures, and expertises, and that these should be preserved. In particular, the strengthening of cooperation should not be in the direction of transforming the IMF into a channel for long-term finance or of shifting the IBRD away from its primary focus on development financing. The Deputies agree that improved cooperation between the two institutions does not require institutional changes, formal rules, or rigid procedures. Several operational proposals were examined by the Deputies in this connection. They recommend that the implementation of these proposals should be considered by the Executive Boards of the two institutions.

93. A first group of proposals concerns ways to achieve closer contacts and exchanges between the two institutions at both management and staff levels. In particular, representatives of one institution could attend board meetings of the other when the discussion concerns countries where both institutions have programs; staff of one institution could participate in the missions of the other; and, more generally, the two institutions could maintain a continuous exchange of information on country analysis and their activities. On occasion, joint meetings of the two Boards or joint seminars or working groups on topics of common interest could be held. Finally, the pooling of some facilities, notably training activities, research programs, and data bases, as well as local representation, could be considered.

94. A second group of proposals addresses the need to ensure greater consistency in program objectives and instruments. In this regard, the Deputies stress that it is important for the two institutions to contribute, each from its own standpoint, to a consistent assessment of medium-term projections of external financial positions and economic developments and policies. In this context, greater coordination of the financial support provided by the two institutions should also be sought, particularly where a reduction in access to IMF credit might be accompanied by appropriate forms of increased IBRD lending.

95. Finally, as regards the IBRD's activities, the Deputies note that while program lending will continue to increase, primary emphasis must remain on project lending. They stress that the conditionality of IBRD lending should not be weakened. At the same time, they believe that the IBRD should be more active in encouraging external finance for investment, supporting medium-term structural adjustment, and enhancing its role as aid coordinator in developing countries.

## Chapter VI: Summary and Conclusions

### General Considerations

96. The Deputies have conducted a thorough review of the international monetary system, with the aim of identifying the areas for progressive improvements in its functioning. Their review has focused in particular on the exchange rate system, international surveillance, international liquidity, and the role of the IMF.

97. The Deputies have concluded that the basic structure of the present system, as reflected in the Articles of Agreement of the IMF, has provided the essential flexibility for individual nations and the international community as a whole to respond constructively to a period of major adjustment to global change. They agree that the fundamental approach of the Articles remains valid and that the key elements of the current international monetary system require no major institutional change.

98. The Deputies recognize, however, that the international monetary system has also shown weaknesses and that there is a need to improve its functioning in order to foster greater stability by promoting convergence of economic performances through the adoption of sound and compatible policies in IMF member countries. The conclusions of the Deputies are based on this approach and call for enhanced cooperation and a stronger role for the IMF.

### The Exchange Rate System

99. The Deputies agree that the present exchange rate system based on the floating of key currencies has shown strengths but also weaknesses. Flexible exchange rates among the major currencies have made a positive contribution to the adjustment process and to the maintenance and growth of international trade and payments in a difficult global environment. How-

ever, there have been both a high degree of short-term volatility of nominal exchange rates and large medium-term swings in real exchange rates due mainly to unsound policies and divergent performance, as well as to adverse external developments. The Deputies agree that such conditions are a potential threat to the open trading and payments system, and that greater exchange rate stability is desirable.

**100.** The Group of Ten Ministers and Governors have already concluded that a return to a generalized system of fixed parities is unrealistic at the present time. In the view of the large majority of the Deputies, the adoption of alternatives to a system based on the floating of key currencies is unrealistic under current and foreseeable circumstances. All Deputies agree, however, that improvements are needed in the functioning of the present system.

**101.** While their study of the functioning of the exchange rate system has focused primarily on the objective of achieving greater stability among the floating currencies, the Deputies are fully aware that attempts to maintain exchange rates at levels not in line with economic fundamentals and market forces can be very damaging, both to the countries concerned and to their trading partners. They have expressed their strong support for efforts regularly made by the IMF to persuade countries to adopt realistic exchange rate policies.

**102.** The Deputies agree that the achievement of greater exchange rate stability would require close and continuing cooperation among major countries. In particular, they emphasize the following:

i) an essential condition of exchange rate stability is convergence of economic performance in the direction of sustainable non-inflationary growth;

ii) this in turn requires not only sound, consistent policies but also the removal of artificial barriers and structural rigidities which inhibit market flexibility;

iii) the international implications and interactions of domestic economic policies should be given close attention in the domestic policymaking process and in international consultations;

iv) a wide range of factors, including developments in exchange rates, fiscal and monetary policies, structural rigidities, and barriers to international trade and capital flows should be taken into account in determining the need for consultations and policy discussion;

v) the role of exchange market intervention can only be a limited one, as intervention will normally be useful only when complementing and supporting other appropriate policies. However, intervention can be useful to counter disorderly market conditions and reduce short-term volatility. Countries should be willing to undertake coordinated intervention on occasions when it is agreed that it would be helpful.

**103.** Some Deputies have proposed the introduction of target zones for exchange rates as more formal and binding indicators for the conduct of macroeconomic policies, maintaining that convergence of economic performance, while necessary, may not always be sufficient to achieve lasting exchange rate stability. Some other Deputies recognize there could be merits in this proposal and suggest that the technical aspects of a target zone approach should be further explored at an appropriate time. The majority of the Deputies, however, consider that such a move would be undesirable and in any case impractical in current circumstances.

## Surveillance

**104.** In considering ways to promote the convergence of economic performances toward sustainable non-inflationary growth through the adoption of sound, compatible policies, the Deputies have agreed that surveillance, especially by the IMF, is the basic tool for moving toward these objectives. They recall that the amended Article IV of the Articles of Agreement gives the IMF increased responsibility to exercise firm surveillance over the exchange rate policies in order to ensure that members fulfill their obligations inter alia to:

i) pursue economic and financial policies aimed at orderly economic growth with reasonable price stability;

ii) foster underlying economic and financial conditions that do not tend to produce erratic disruptions;

iii) avoid manipulating exchange rates or the international monetary system to prevent effective balance of payments adjustment or to gain an unfair competitive advantage.

**105.** For this purpose, the IMF has developed principles and procedures for surveillance which have been implemented and evolved over time. The Deputies recognize, however, that it would be necessary to strengthen the substance and procedures of surveillance to maximize its potential usefulness. To this end they suggest that:

i) the surveillance process should involve the senior level in governments in order to have an impact on policymaking;

ii) possibilities for public scrutiny playing an increased role in the surveillance process should be explored;

iii) governments should be more ready to take other countries' advice into account, and the policy discussions of the surveillance process should allow greater emphasis on the international interaction and repercussions of policies, the working of the international adjustment process, and the progress of convergence of economic performances of major countries.

**106.** The Deputies recommend that the IMF consider the following steps to strengthen surveillance:

**i)** increasing the ability of the Managing Director and the staff to bring international concerns to the attention of members by the following measures:

**(a)** a confidential exchange of views between the Managing Director and the Finance Minister should be envisaged at the end of the consultation process in the case of industrial and developing countries whose policies and performance are of greatest concern for the world economy;

**(b)** participation in Article IV consultation should be at an appropriately high level, and the IMF report and summing-up should be brought to the attention of key economic policymakers;

**ii)** making more candid assessments and proposals for policy changes and, when necessary, follow-up reports to the Executive Board on actions taken by the member to respond to IMF suggestions;

**iii)** broadening the scope of Article IV documents to provide certain additional information and analysis;

**iv)** making greater use of the supplemental surveillance procedures in the face of exchange rate and other developments that may be important or may have important effects on other members, or that have implications for the operation of the international monetary system. The Deputies invite the IMF to review the relevant decisions for invoking these procedures;

**v)** continuing to develop "enhanced" surveillance procedures to be applied on a case-by-case basis at the request of members, with the aim of facilitating non-IMF financing in connection with multiyear debt rescheduling or in cases where IMF assistance and advice would improve the member's limited access to external finance.

**107.** The Deputies have agreed that new arrangements for multilateral surveillance should be introduced to promote greater consistency of policies among countries in order to provide the basis for greater exchange market stability. They recommend that:

**i)** the IMF periodically prepare as a special chapter of the World Economic Outlook (WEO) an expanded analysis of the international repercussions of national policies of Group of Ten countries and of their interaction in influencing exchange rate developments and international adjustment;

**ii)** the Group of Ten Ministers and Governors contribute to the process of multilateral surveillance by cooperating with the IMF in reviewing, under appropriate procedures, the policies and performances of Group of Ten countries as well as the policy recommendations of the special chapter of the WEO.

## International Liquidity

**108.** The Deputies have concentrated their attention on the supply and distribution of international liquidity by international capital markets and official channels. They have agreed that the liberalization and integration of national capital markets have permitted a significant increase in international capital flows and enhanced the ability of creditworthy countries to meet their financing needs, although some countries continue to have little or no access to capital markets. While creditworthiness of borrowers will continue to be the principal factor in determining access to financial markets, the Deputies recognize that the availability and cost of liquidity are also affected by factors such as interest rates and credit policies in major countries. The combination of these factors does not necessarily ensure that the requirements of the international monetary and financial system are met.

**109.** In order to improve the stability of the international monetary system, the Deputies have agreed that it would be desirable to avoid excessive swings in the availability of liquidity. To this end they have reached a consensus on the need:

**i)** to improve the creditworthiness of debtor countries by encouraging economic adjustment;

**ii)** to improve IMF surveillance over the policies of countries which affect the availability and terms of credit in international financial markets; such surveillance is an integral part of the broad surveillance process on exchange rate policies and should be implemented in a closely integrated manner with other aspects of surveillance;

**iii)** to deregulate further capital markets and liberalize capital movements;

**iv)** for monetary authorities to pay due regard in the monitoring process of international banking activities to possible macroeconomic consequences of prudential measures;

**v)** to maintain the ability of the IMF to respond to systemic liquidity problems;

**vi)** to provide official finance on appropriate terms to developing countries which, despite adjustment efforts, lack sufficient access to capital markets.

**110.** The Deputies have reviewed the role of the SDR. They recognize that the international monetary system has changed considerably since the original creation of the SDR scheme and that this has affected the rationale for the SDR, including the objective of placing the SDR at the center of the system as the main reserve asset.

**111.** The Deputies have discussed both normal SDR allocations and other ideas for developing the SDR, but found no consensus within the Group on any specific proposal. However, they recognize that the

SDR may still have a useful role in meeting the long-term global need for reserves and in this context in providing a safety net for future contingencies. In these circumstances, the Deputies support the intention of the IMF Executive Directors to carry out a comprehensive review of the future role of the SDR in the system.

## The Role of the IMF

112. The Deputies recognize that the IMF has played a vital role in promoting international financial stability and external adjustment. They stress the need to safeguard its monetary character and the revolving nature of its financing, as well as the importance of keeping it as a quota-based financial institution and its lending normally in line with quota resources. They also stress the need to continue to phase down the policy of enlarged access and to terminate it as soon as the situation of external payments permits, and to deal with the problem of prolonged use and arrears.

113. The Deputies underline that IMF conditionality plays an essential role in encouraging adjustment and the restoration of creditworthiness. They stress the importance of maintaining the effectiveness of conditionality in order for the IMF to promote sound conditions in the world economic and financial system. They also stress that IMF credit should be available on a sufficient scale to provide meaningful support to members and to serve as an important catalyst for other lending by providing confidence that the borrower is pursuing sound policies.

114. The Deputies agree that, barring unforeseen circumstances, the recent increase in IMF quotas and the enlargement and expansion of the GAB provide the institution with an adequate basis to fulfill its responsibilities over the next few years. However, they recognize that negotiations on quotas and borrowing arrangements are complex and time consuming. They therefore suggest that the IMF undertake a study of alternative techniques that would provide resources to deal with exceptional circumstances without involving an immediate increase in members' subscriptions, thus adding to the operational flexibility of the institution.

115. Finally, the Deputies recognize that a number of countries are facing both macroeconomic and structural difficulties which result in balance of payments problems, and that cooperation between the IMF and the IBRD should therefore be strengthened to address these problems in a coordinated manner, without jeopardizing the unique purposes of each institution. They recommend that the Executive Boards of the IMF and the IBRD continue their efforts to ensure that policy advice and the provision of financial resources by the two institutions be coordinated more than in the past, particularly where a reduction in access to IMF credit might be accompanied by appropriate forms of increased IBRD lending. The Deputies have also reviewed a number of specific proposals and recommend that they be submitted to the Executive Boards for consideration.

# Appendix II
# Report of the Deputies of the Group of Twenty-Four: The Functioning and Improvement of the International Monetary System

## Chapter I: Summary of Recommendations

1. This Report has made a number of recommendations in the major areas of concern for the international monetary system which are summarized in paragraphs below.

### The Functioning of the Present Exchange Rate System

2. The experience with the present exchange rate system has not been satisfactory. Exchange rates of major currencies were characterized by a high degree of short-term volatility as well as persistent misalignment which brought about uncertainty regarding future exchange rates, discouraged investment and trade, and resulted in misallocation of resources.

3. Volatility and misalignment of exchange rates have especially hurt the developing countries. They severely affected trade and raised reserve needs of these countries.

4. Exchange rate stability should be an important objective of policy, instead of being a residual of other policy actions of individual countries, as is the case at present. It is necessary to devise an exchange rate system to overcome the recognized rigidities of the par value system and the destabilizing uncertainties of floating rates.

5. The principle behind the concept of "target zones" for exchange rates of major industrial countries, commitment to which would promote greater international policy consistency, is in line with the approach of the 1984 Group of Twenty-Four Revised Program. Adoption of target zones for the exchange rates of major currencies could help achieve the objective of exchange rate stability and sustainable levels of payments balances. The proposal needs to be further studied and pursued in order to gain general acceptance. In the meantime, a mechanism has to be devised to enforce policy coordination among the major industrial countries.

6. Policy coordination among major industrial countries would imply complementary use of monetary, fiscal, and other policy instruments consistent with exchange rate stability and growth without inflation. Intervention may have to be used as a supplementary device for stabilizing exchange rates.

7. A framework for policy coordination already exists under the IMF Articles. In addition to that, a mechanism to trigger consultations among the concerned countries and the Fund is necessary whenever the indicators available suggest excessive short-term movements or misalignments of major currencies. In determining misalignment, the focal point of concern should not be just the attainment of balance in international payments but achieving the objectives of expansion and balanced growth of international trade with high levels of employment and real income and a durable payments equilibrium. The Fund should concentrate more than in the past on issues of a systemic character, and all coordination of policies should take account of the needs of developing countries.

8. Exchange rates of individual developing countries do not have any systemic impact on international alignment of exchange rates. Assessment of the appropriateness of a developing country's exchange rate is not comparable with considerations that are applicable to the exchange rate of a major industrial country.

### Surveillance

9. The surveillance function of the IMF is crucial for an orderly international monetary and financial system. It has so far been largely ineffective on major industrial countries, resulting in asymmetry in the international adjustment process, the burden of which has fallen disproportionately on developing countries. The main

objectives of Fund surveillance should be to bring about symmetric international adjustment and facilitate expansion and balanced growth of international trade, high economic growth, and orderly financial conditions. To achieve these objectives, Fund surveillance should effectively influence the policies of industrial countries in a manner that would be supportive of growth, particularly of developing countries.

10. Multilateral surveillance and bilateral (Article IV) consultations should form two separate stages of the surveillance process. The first stage would involve multilateral negotiations about a mutually consistent set of objectives and policies among the major industrial countries. These multilateral negotiations should be conducted on a regular basis within the framework of the IMF. The World Economic Outlook exercise should provide the background for multilateral consultations, spelling out the international repercussions of national policies of major industrial countries. The second stage would involve a comparison between the actual outcomes and the targets of policy, setting off discussions of appropriate measures when the two deviate. The Fund should follow up with reports on recommended policies and performance indicators and deviations from them. These reports should be discussed by the Fund Board.

11. For improving effectiveness of surveillance over industrial countries, it is necessary to continuously monitor key developments pertaining to these countries and exercise pressure on them during both multilateral surveillance and Article IV consultations.

12. Bilateral consultations with major industrial countries should evaluate their policies against this multilateral framework of international adjustment. If the Board is not convinced of a country's explanations for the deviations from the recommended policies, it could request the Managing Director of the Fund to discuss the matter further with the country concerned and to report back to the Board the outcome of these discussions for appropriate action.

13. For major industrial countries, Article IV consultations should concentrate on a thorough assessment of their national policies and their international impact. For developing countries, recommendations of policies should be made with a view to promoting adjustment consistent with economic development, bringing out the underlying needs of finance and the part that exogenous factors play on the adjustment efforts of these countries.

14. In prescribing exchange rate policies for developing countries, it is essential to consider that changes in resource allocation are time consuming and would need adequate financing. In many developing countries, controls to limit capital outflows may become necessary for the stability of exchange and interest rates. Flexibility in regard to use of multiple currency practices is also necessary in certain cases.

15. In view of the underlying confidentiality of the exchange of information and discussion between the members and the Fund, no publicity should be given to the conclusions of the consultations in any form.

16. The Fund should continue to play its role in easing the debt burden of developing countries through arrangements for use of Fund resources and also in a catalytic manner for facilitating the flow of resources from banks and other creditors. Deputies expressed concern over the implications of IMF involvement in "enhanced surveillance." It is viewed by the Deputies as yet another evidence of creditor unwillingness to restore normal access to external financing despite significant adjustment efforts. The catalytic role of the IMF should, in principle, be exercised without "enhanced surveillance." However, in cases where it proves necessary "enhanced surveillance" should be considered exceptional and undertaken only at the request of a member country. It is justified only if it secures financing from non-Fund sources in the context of a multiyear debt rescheduling. It is important that in "enhanced surveillance," priority is given to policies aimed at promoting self-sustained growth. However, the Fund's continued analysis and policy advice under "enhanced surveillance" arrangements should be clearly differentiated from the programs under Fund arrangements. The main objective of "enhanced surveillance" should be the early normalization of market relations between the member country and the international financial system. To this end, the period under which the country is under "enhanced surveillance" should be limited to the debt consolidation period or the grace period.

## Management of International Liquidity and the SDR

17. The record of creation and management of international liquidity in the past decade has been unsatisfactory. During this period the supply of international liquidity was uneven and grossly inadequate, especially for developing countries. The recent contraction in commercial bank lending shows its unreliability as a source of liquidity.

18. Even if certain improvements in the functioning of capital markets such as deregulation are brought about, they may not result in increased availability of credit to developing countries. The recent improvement in the balance of payments of many of these countries has not reversed the decline in commercial lending to them, despite strenuous adjustment efforts.

19. If reserves are to be built to acquire "creditwor-

thiness," many developing countries will be required to generate current account surpluses for the next several years, at a time when many of them are facing a severe problem of reverse flows of real resources. For low-income countries, the official assistance fell in real terms in recent years, and they face a severe shortage of liquidity. As a result, many of these countries have accumulated payments arrears. They have to approach the Fund for support but often have to face reduced access limits and tightened conditionality without the provision of adequate liquidity.

20. The conditions of supply of international liquidity and its distribution are more important than the world aggregate reserve holdings. The scope for international liquidity policy is now limited by the willingness of major countries to consider the international impact of their policies. In addition to surveillance over exchange rate and other macroeconomic policies of major industrial countries, the Fund should be enabled to influence the liquidity of the world economy through adequate SDR creation and its more efficient distribution.

21. There is at present a long-term global need for a substantial allocation of SDRs in relation to expected growth of world trade, financial transactions, and output. An allocation at this time would relieve the stringency in the reserve position of a large number of developing countries; promote economic recovery and not be inflationary; improve balance between conditional and unconditional liquidity; reduce dependence on costly borrowed resources; and help orderly adjustment. For this purpose, an annual allocation of no less than SDR 15 billion as recommended by the 1984 Group of Twenty-Four Revised Program is warranted.

22. To make the SDR the principal reserve asset, as required under the Articles, SDRs should be issued on a regular annual basis with a view to ensuring that their proportion in reserves rises progressively.

23. Since the unsatisfied liquidity needs of developing countries are more than those of industrial countries, distribution of supply of liquidity in favor of developing countries would benefit all countries without creating any additional inflationary pressures. It will be desirable to link the allocation of SDRs to the development needs of developing countries.

## Role of the IMF

24. The purposes of the International Monetary Fund were set out in Article I of the Articles of Agreement. During the past forty years, the Fund has certainly played an important role, but it was not very successful in fulfilling the aspirations of a large number of developing countries, which form a substantial part of the Fund membership.

25. The Fund has a role to play both in financing transitory payments problems and in financing and promoting adjustment of persistent imbalances.

26. Transitory payments problems are met by international reserves, borrowing from capital markets, or drawing on Fund resources. The compensatory financing facility (CFF) was created to provide low conditionality finance to meet transitory payments deficits produced by events outside the control of the borrowing country. The effectiveness of this facility has been in the recent past very much diluted. The tighter conditionality attached to the CFF and the reduction of access limits are retrograde steps and should be reversed immediately. The CFF should be extended to cover not only export shortfalls but also deterioration in terms of trade that is quantifiable. CFF drawings should be related to calculated shortfalls rather than to quotas, and should be provided automatically. The repayment period of the CFF should be extended as recessions have tended to become deeper and the cycles longer in the recent past, giving rise to prolonged stress on the balances of payments of most developing countries.

27. In view of the large variability in interest rates, a new facility to provide financing for interest rate increases needs to be introduced. This facility could also be a part of a facility which may cover deficit resulting from any exogenous factor that is reversible.

28. In contrast to transitory imbalances, persistent payment deficits require both large-scale finance and adjustment. The Fund is enjoined to promote adjustment with due regard to the requirements of growth and prosperity. Therefore, adjustment measures should not lead to contraction in activities and reduction of growth and development in the deficit countries.

29. Policies to correct persistent imbalances should be devised according to the nature of the underlying disequilibrium. Persistent disequilibria in developing countries are often structural in nature, requiring measures to raise the economy's productive capacity and expand the supply of goods and services.

30. Reorientation of conditionality criteria from demand deflation to growth-oriented structural adjustment requires lengthened program periods and increased levels of financing. Instead of underplaying the EFF (extended Fund facility) as in the past two years, it should be used extensively.

31. It is recognized that the balance of payments problems of most low-income countries are structural in nature, caused mainly by persistent deterioration in their terms of trade, disproportionately large debt-service burden, decline in the flow of ODA (official development assistance), and very limited capability

to attract external resources from non-official sources. These problems have been seriously compounded by devastating droughts of unprecedented proportions that have hit many African countries. Of late, many low-income countries have experienced net outflows of resources, including to the multilateral financial institutions. In view of the particularly difficult structural problems of these countries, it is essential that the Fund provide substantially larger and longer-term financing in support of their structural adjustment programs than has been done so far.

32. Some Fund programs have broken down in recent years because of excessively rigid performance criteria, which were not revised in the light of unforeseen developments beyond the control of the borrowing country. There is a need for greater flexibility in the application of such criteria. It is necessary that repayment obligations to the Fund are settled on time. However, where the balance of payments situation, made adverse by exogenous factors, makes it practically impossible for a country to repay according to a fixed schedule, mechanical application of sanctions would not be appropriate. To help such countries become current in their obligations to the Fund, new mechanisms should be evolved, in collaboration with the World Bank and regional development institutions, to provide longer-term assistance for orderly adjustment of these countries.

33. In recent years, the burden of increase in costs of Fund activities has fallen disproportionately on developing countries. Increasing rates of charge and the declining grant element impaired the process of adjustment, especially in low-income countries. To alleviate this, facilities and mechanisms should be established in the Fund, such as an Interest Subsidy Account on a stable basis. The Trust Fund should be revived to make concessional loans to eligible countries.

34. Quotas must remain the primary source of finance for the Fund. The Eighth Review of Quotas has fallen far short of the current requirements, which underlines the need to advance the Ninth Review. It would be desirable to relate quotas to a measure of the size of the world economy. In the absence of such a link, the interval of quota reviews should be reduced to three years. Until the size of quotas is increased adequately the option of borrowing by the Fund from any other official source should be kept open.

35. Enlarged Access Policy should be continued until the size of quotas bears an appropriate relationship to the size of the world economy. The present limits of access are too meager and should be enhanced to be useful for orderly adjustment in developing countries.

36. Any coordination between the Fund and the World Bank should not lead to cross conditionality, but should help further their mutual objective of providing resources to developing countries. While closer contacts between the management and staff of both institutions and sharing of relevant information could be useful, steps to seek uniformity of advice should not become a means of exerting a concerted pressure on the borrowing countries.

37. The role of developing countries in the decision-making process in the international financial institutions needs to be substantially increased. The system of weighted voting has led to a situation where, after the Eight Quota Review, developing countries as a group have no more than 38 percent of total votes. While the principle of weighted voting may be unavoidable in financial institutions, a better balance in the voting pattern is needed for a more equitable and effective functioning of these institutions. The share of developing countries in the total votes in the multilateral financial institutions should be increased to 50 percent. For this purpose, consideration might be given to, inter alia, an increase in basic votes. The present geographical representation of developing country regions in the Boards of the Bank and the Fund should be preserved.

## The Debt Problem and Transfer of Resources

38. The debtor countries have been undertaking strenuous adjustment efforts in response to the external environment and the consequential adjustment process is having serious social and political consequences. The debt crisis is a result of excessive lending by commercial banks, abrupt policy changes, and, in some cases, an unbalanced policy mix by industrial countries and other factors leading to historically high interest rates, excessive borrowing with inadequate policies by many debtor countries, and the failure of Fund programs in the case of many low-income countries. Thus, finding realistic formulae and viable mechanisms for the solution of the crisis would require cooperative actions of debtor and creditor countries, commercial banks, and multilateral financial institutions. It is important to reiterate the view of the Group of Twenty-Four Ministers, as expressed in their April 1985 communique: "Also required is a co-responsibility of debtors and creditors, symmetry of adjustment, and cooperative efforts aimed at a durable solution to the debt problem in a global framework."

39. The debt situation requires imaginative solutions involving debt restructuring and relief in order to bring the debt burden within the effective ability of the debtor countries to pay. There is an urgent need to move toward a "positive" type of adjustment, con-

sistent with sustained growth of output in the medium and the long run. To support the efforts by developing countries to prevent the capital flight from the debtor countries, developed countries should, through their regulatory agencies, discourage capital outflows from those developing countries which are facing acute capital flight problems. Multiyear restructuring of debts has prevented the bunching of maturities in the near future and has been a helpful development. Co-responsibility of debtors and creditors also requires that interest rates should more closely reflect the real cost of funds for the creditors.

**40.** The lesson learned from the recent experience with the debt crisis is that heavy reliance on medium- and short-term borrowing for development financing is bound to give rise to liquidity problems even if such financing were to be directed to sound and viable projects. Therefore, there is an imperative need to expand sufficiently the resource base of international institutions.

**41.** In recognition of the interdependence of money, finance, and trade in the global economy, it is important to emphasize the close relationship between an expanding world trade and the solution of balance of payments problems, including the indebtedness of developing countries. Developed countries should therefore roll back protectionist measures, refrain from introducing new restrictions, and improve access for exports of developing countries to their markets.

**42.** Adequate flows of long-term resources are of paramount importance to the orderly and speedy adjustment of developing countries. The official flows in recent years have not even made up for the losses incurred by the developing countries on account of adverse movements of terms of trade and high interest rates. The quality and composition of aid also deteriorated.

**43.** The IDA (International Development Association) has played an important role in promoting development and increasing productivity, thus helping to raise the standard of living and to alleviate poverty in the low-income countries. There has been a steep decline in IDA resources in the Seventh Replenishment, and additional commitments are necessary. During the mid-term review to be conducted shortly by the IDA, additional resources should be made available to restore the IDA VII Replenishment to US$12 billion. It is essential that funding for IDA VIII should be substantially larger than that for IDA VI, and efforts should be made to restore the historical rates of growth in IDA. The Special Assistance Facility established for sub-Saharan Africa is inadequate and it will be necessary to substantially increase the level and quality of funding in this respect. Developed countries should redouble their efforts to reach the internationally agreed target of 0.7 percent of GNP (gross national product) as official development assistance as quickly as possible and at any rate not later than the end of this decade. Each developed country should make binding commitments for annual growth rate of assistance. In respect of low-income countries, the Resolution of the Trade and Development Board 165 (S-IX) should be implemented expeditiously and fully.

**44.** The role of the World Bank should continue to be one of commitment to development, growth, and poverty alleviation. The recent reduction in the lending program of the Bank is regrettable and it is essential to adopt lending policies to enable it to provide effective support. It is also urgently necessary to increase the general capital of the World Bank to resume significant increases in flows to developing countries. In this context it is disturbing to note that there is a possibility of negative net transfers from the World Bank, and this should be reversed effectively. The Bank's lending policies including those of structural adjustment should conform to the national policy requirements of the borrowing countries. There should not be undue emphasis on so-called policy-based lending or on linking the quantum of Bank assistance to increasing conditionality.

## Follow-up Action

**45.** The recommendations of the Deputies of the Group of Twenty-Four embodied in this Report, together with those of the Group of Ten, should receive consideration by the Interim Committee in October 1985. But, as the assessment of the situation in the world economy by developing countries differs from that by industrial countries, with different policy implications, a suitable institutional mechanism should be evolved for an in-depth and joint examination of the two Reports. A representative committee of Ministers from developing and industrial countries, which could perhaps take the form of a joint subcommittee of both the Interim and Development Committees, should be formed for this purpose. It should conduct its business on the basis of consensus.

## Chapter II: Introduction

**46.** The Ministers of the Group of Twenty-Four adopted, in September 1984, the *Revised Program of Action Towards Reform of the International Monetary and Financial System* (hereafter referred to as 1984 Group of Twenty-Four Revised Program), which examined the various shortcomings of the international monetary and financial system and made several recommendations to improve its functioning.

47. The continued malfunctioning of the international monetary and financial system has also led to repeated calls from the nonaligned countries, the Group of 77, and several important industrial countries for the examination, in a broad-based international forum, of the defects of the existing system. They underlined the need for action for improvement and reform of the system.

48. The Interim Committee, at its meeting on April 17–19, 1985, noted that improvements in the international monetary system were currently under study and agreed to review this matter at its next meeting in Seoul. The Ministers representing the Group of Ten have recently forwarded a Report of their Deputies on the Functioning of the International Monetary System for the consideration of the Interim Committee. That Report covers mainly four areas, namely, the exchange rate system, surveillance, international liquidity, and the role of the Fund.

49. In May 1985, the Chairman of the Group of Twenty-Four appointed a Working Group to examine these and some other related issues in the light of recent developments. The report of the Working Group was examined by the Deputies of the Group of Twenty-Four and it forms the basis of this Report.

50. The Deputies wish to emphasize that the 1984 Group of Twenty-Four Revised Program . . . sets out the basic position of the Group on various issues of the international monetary and financial system. This Report is essentially an elaboration of the Revised Program on the areas covered in the Group of Ten Report and also the problems of debt and transfer of resources, as no meaningful improvement of the international monetary system is possible without their solution.

51. The recommendations of the Deputies of the Group of Twenty-Four embodied in this Report, together with those of the Group of Ten, should receive consideration by the Interim Committee in October 1985. But, as the assessment of the situation in the world economy by developing countries differs from that by industrial countries, with different policy implications, a suitable institutional mechanism should be evolved for an in-depth and joint examination of the two Reports. A representative committee of Ministers from developing and industrial countries, which could perhaps take the form of a joint subcommittee of both the Interim and Development Committees, should be formed for this purpose. It should conduct its business on the basis of consensus.

52. The Group of Twenty-Four Deputies considered that an effective reform of the international monetary and financial system requires a convening of an international conference. The joint examination of the recommendations of these Reports by the proposed representative committee of Ministers will be an effective step in preparing for such a conference.

## Chapter III: An Overview of the International Economic Situation

53. The low growth rates and severe recessionary conditions in the international economy that prevailed in the early 1980s continue to have debilitating effects on many developing countries. The recovery in industrial countries, which showed its first signs in 1983 and peaked in 1984, has been fragile, partial, and unbalanced. Unemployment has remained high. And there has been intensification of current account imbalances of a number of industrial countries. Disparities in their fiscal stance, too, have continued. There has also been a deceleration in the growth of trade in recent months. In 1985 so far, the rate of expansion in these countries has slowed down considerably and the growth rate in the current year will perhaps be one half of the 4.9 percent rate recorded in 1984. The medium-term scenarios until the end of the decade, as set out in the World Economic Outlook for 1985, envisage that the average rate of growth in industrial countries will be slightly over 3 percent.

54. Per capita real incomes of many developing countries continue to be lower than in the 1970s. Most of them have large current account deficits, and large debts to be serviced. Their capacity to repay by generating export surpluses is limited not only by their own low growth performance but also by declines in the terms of trade, an increase in protectionism, and the low growth in industrial countries. Prices of oil, primary commodities, and manufactures of developing countries have either declined or been falling. The index for non-oil commodity prices in June 1985 is about 30 percent below the 1980 average and is lower than the bottom level recorded in 1982. High real interest rates have increased the debt service burden further. Interest rates ruled high during a good part of the 1980s. There has, however, been a welcome decline in interest rates in recent months, but with the spreads for "country risks" and with falling export prices, the real interest rate payable on bank loans by debtor countries would be unsustainable in the long run as it may exceed the likely rate of growth in real income and the real value of exports.

55. Official assistance and Fund financial support have both declined. Commercial bank lending to developing countries has been virtually withdrawn since the middle of 1982. The value of "spontaneous" syndicated credits raised by developing countries at $10.9 billion in 1984 was lower than $14.2 billion in 1983. In the first five months of 1985, no more than $2.9 billion was

raised, indicating a continuation of the downward trend.

**56.** The net effect of these developments is that there has been a substantial outflow of resources from many developing economies. If this situation continues, the stability of the international financial system would be seriously impaired, unless the international community takes immediate steps to correct it in a manner that promotes adjustment and growth in developing countries. In the case of low-income countries, viability in external accounts and future development could be brought about only by substantial concessional financing.

**57.** Correction of the present malady requires a concerted action on the part of the policymakers in the industrial countries and in the major international institutions. The functioning of the exchange rate system should be improved to reflect fundamental underlying economic conditions. To ensure consistent policies among industrial countries aimed at sustained growth and financial and exchange rate stability, Fund surveillance of major industrial countries should be strengthened. The IMF should promote an international monetary system in which payments adjustment fosters international prosperity. Adjustment by strong demand management policies has in the past led to contractionary situations in many developing countries. Further adjustment of this kind in the present circumstances would sap their growth potential, reduce their imports, and ultimately bring about a fall in the volume of trade. Adjustment without large-scale financing would not, in the current circumstances, lead to correction of persistent payments imbalances. And inadequate financing with high conditionality would correct neither transitory nor persistent payments imbalances.

**58.** Developing countries suffer from a shortage of resources for productive investment activities. They have large reserve requirements. Their liquidity needs will have to be met by substantial SDR allocations, which will promote trade expansion without endangering price stability. Their development programs will have to be supported by large international financing. Even their balance of payments adjustment programs should be supported with substantial medium-term financing by the international institutions. But, in order to enable countries to approach these institutions, conditionality in lending should be modified by bringing forward development as a major objective. In turn, to enable these international institutions to play their part, their resources should be strengthened by increasing their quotas/general capital, and access of borrowers to these resources should be enhanced. The absence of adequate financing, in fact, could take the world economy back to the recessionary conditions.

## Chapter IV: The Functioning of the Present Exchange Rate System

**59.** Floating exchange rates were adopted by major industrial countries in the early seventies, as the par value system established at Bretton Woods could not cope with the stresses generated by divergent national macroeconomic policies in an environment of increasing capital mobility. It had been anticipated at that time that market forces, aided by stabilizing capital flows, would keep exchange rates close to the levels required to achieve current account equilibrium and free other macroeconomic instruments to deal with domestic economic priorities. It was also hoped that floating exchange rates would assist the adjustment process and growth of world trade and output.

## The Experience with Floating Rates

**60.** The experience with floating exchange rates has not been up to the original expectations. Both in terms of short-term volatility and long-term misalignment, exchange rate variability has increased since the abandonment of the Bretton Woods system. The increase in volatility, referring to short-term fluctuations, since the adoption of floating rates is well documented. Exchange rate volatility has not declined as markets became used to dealing with the flexible exchange rate system, as was anticipated when floating was first adopted.

**61.** Wide fluctuations in exchange rates have tended to bring about greater uncertainty about future exchange rates. Evidence from forward markets indicates that most exchange rate fluctuations are unanticipated. Volatility has contributed to expansion of financial transactions and greater capital movements not directly related to trade flows. It has discouraged investment and trade by adding to financial risks for investors and traders.

**62.** Misalignment, referring to a persistent deviation of the exchange rate from the equilibrium level, has been severe and, according to some studies, it has also become larger in the recent period than under the Bretton Woods system. Much of the medium-term movement in real exchange rates in recent years reflects not the changing pattern of competitiveness but rather the result of differences in fiscal and monetary policies, in which industrial countries have chosen macroeconomic policies independently, without serious consideration of their impact on the world economy. Misalignment inevitably produces either idle resources or wasteful shifts of resources back and forth between tradables and nontradables. It becomes a potent source of pressures for protectionism.

63. Exchange rate variability has, as the 1984 Group of Twenty-Four Revised Program had put it, "especially hurt the developing countries." Exporters and importers in these countries are exposed to high exchange risks in the absence of well-developed financial markets, especially forward cover arrangements. The destabilizing uncertainties of floating rates have increased the reserve and capital needs of developing countries from the levels which would otherwise exist.

64. The functioning of the present floating-rate system has thus not been able to provide, as Article IV, Section 1 of the Articles of Agreement of the IMF puts it, "a framework that facilitates the exchange of goods, services, and capital among countries," which sustains sound economic growth and helps develop orderly underlying conditions necessary for financial and economic stability.

## Proposals for Improving Exchange Rate Stability

65. The 1984 Group of Twenty-Four Revised Program stated that an exchange rate system should be devised to overcome the recognized rigidities of a par value system and the destabilizing uncertainties of floating rates. Besides, the improved functioning of the exchange rate system requires the recognition by major countries that both the floating-rate and the fixed-rate systems need rules of the game relating to domestic macroeconomic policies. The Revised Program categorically stated that "this implies greater effort on the part of the developed countries to achieve a substantial degree of discipline and coordination in the conduct of their national policies." Exchange rate stability should be an important objective of policy instead of being a residual of other policy actions of individual countries, as is the case at present.

66. The principle behind the concept of "target zones" for exchange rates of major countries, commitment to which would promote greater international policy consistency, is in line with the approach of the 1984 Group of Twenty-Four Revised Program. Adoption of target zones for the exchange rates of major currencies could help achieve the objective of exchange rate stability and a sustainable pattern of payments balances. The proposal needs to be further studied and pursued to gain general acceptance. In the meantime, a mechanism has to be devised to enforce policy coordination among the developed, especially the key currency, countries. Although the role of the developing countries in influencing such an exchange rate system is necessarily limited—and therefore the related mechanism of coordination and surveillance will be essentially concerned with the developed countries—it is important, as the 1984 Group of Twenty-Four Revised Program states, "that this coordination should take account of the needs of developing countries."

67. Policy coordination in this context implies that monetary policy for exchange rate stability should complement the use of fiscal policy to counter inflationary and deflationary pressures as well as the use of other policy instruments. Intervention, for instance, could be used on a meaningful scale, without confining it to "leaning against the wind," toward the end of exchange rate stability, as a complementary measure to other policies, and sometimes in coordination with other countries.

68. A framework for such a policy coordination already exists under Article IV of the IMF, according to which "each member undertakes to collaborate with the Fund and other members to assure orderly exchange arrangements and to promote a stable system of exchange rates" (Section 1) and "the Fund shall exercise firm surveillance over the exchange rate policies of members, and shall adopt specific principles for the guidance of all members with respect to those policies" (Section 3(*b*)). Over and above the regular multilateral consultations, a mechanism or procedure that would trigger consultations among the concerned countries and between them and the Fund is necessary whenever the indicators available suggest that excessive short-term movements of one or more major currencies are taking place, or that any major currency is already, or is in the process of becoming, seriously misaligned.

69. Since the concept of misalignment is central in this process of surveillance, it should be clearly spelled out in operational terms. Although the term misalignment was not used in 1970, the IMF's report on the "Role of Exchange Rates in the Adjustment of International Payments" of that year provided an authoritative definition of the concept of fundamental disequilibrium, which was the Bretton Woods term for the same thing:

> A basic feature of the concept of fundamental disequilibrium is that although its ultimate focus is on the balance of payments it is related to a general condition of the member's economy and does not require that an imbalance must have developed in the balance of payments. This, in turn, reflects the underlying philosophy of the Bretton Woods system that, while attainment of balance in international payments must be a focal point of concern for the international financial community, it is not to be regarded as an objective in isolation from other objectives of the international monetary system. These objectives include the expansion and balanced growth of international trade on the basis of a liberal and nondiscriminatory regime of trade and payments, to contribute to the promotion of high levels of employment and real income and to the development of the productive resources of all the

Fund's members as primary objectives of economic policy. In this conception, attainment of payments balance through the use of measures destructive of national or international prosperity would clearly not comprise a durable payments equilibrium.

**70.** The alignment or misalignment of an exchange rate thus has to be judged in the light of a country's overall economic performance and its impact on the international economy and not merely its balance of payments performance. For example, in many developing countries with relatively undiversified economies, protection of infant industries, judiciously applied, may be an indispensable element in the process of diversification and development, as recognized by GATT. On the other hand, for countries with diversified economies and relatively high mobility of factors of production, substantial or increasing restrictions on trade could well be a major symptom of exchange rate misalignment.

**71.** Exchange rates of developing countries are not of any great significance in relation to the international alignments of exchange rates, and assessment of the appropriateness of a developing country's exchange rate does not generally involve systemic considerations comparable to those applicable to the exchange rate of a major industrial country.

## Chapter V: Surveillance

**72.** In their 1984 Revised Program, the Group of Twenty-Four Ministers had noted that in view of "the high degree of interdependence of the world economy, the success of economic policy followed by one country often depends on actions by others." It is equally true that cooperative macroeconomic policy formulation on the part of the major industrial countries can achieve a superior outcome for each country, than would be achieved by each acting independently. In the recent past, their uncoordinated attempts to disinflate led to an excessive emphasis being given to monetary restriction relative to other instruments. The result was a halting process of recovery with high real interest rates and low commodity prices having particularly adverse effects on the developing countries.

**73.** The IMF has a key role in the conduct of international surveillance. However, Fund surveillance has to date been largely ineffective over the major industrial countries whose actions have substantial spillover effects on the world economy. These countries have been able to pursue domestic policies without taking into account their impact on the international economy. In some cases, the subordination of international responsibilities to domestic priorities has been quite explicit, and notwithstanding the urgings of the Fund, the mix of monetary and fiscal policies remains inappropriate.

**74.** On the other hand, the influence of the Fund has been effectively felt by the users of its resources, mostly developing countries. Even if a formal distinction is made between Article IV consultations and adjustment programs associated with the use of Fund resources, the effect of Fund surveillance on inducing policy changes is much larger on developing countries than on major industrial countries, which have adequate access to external financing and do not require an IMF-supported adjustment program.

**75.** As a result of this basic asymmetry in the Fund's surveillance function, the international adjustment process has been seriously biased. The deficit developing countries have been faced with harsher adjustment, and the world economy with a lower level of activity, than would otherwise be necessary. Any program for strengthening international surveillance has to reduce this asymmetry and devise methods for coordination of policies of major industrial countries for promoting world economic activity and trade expansion in a manner supportive of growth in developing countries.

## The Objectives of Surveillance

**76.** The objectives of surveillance of the Fund to date are limited to surveillance over members' exchange rate policies. Article IV, Section 3 and Executive Board Decision No. 5392-77/63 (of April 29, 1977) spell out that the Fund shall exercise firm surveillance over the exchange rate policies of members, and that a member shall avoid manipulating exchange rates to prevent effective balance of payments adjustment or to gain an unfair competitive advantage over other members, that it should intervene in the exchange market if necessary to counter disorderly conditions characterized by disruptive short-term movements in the exchange rates, and that it should take into account in its intervention policies the interests of other members.

**77.** Surveillance, to be effective, should be explicitly recognized as surveillance of the international adjustment process. "The adjustment process," stated the 1984 Group of Twenty-Four Revised Program, "must be adapted to the present global economic environment and the need for promoting development." The design of such international adjustment process, based on coordinated national economic policies, must aim at sustained growth of output, employment and trade of all countries and ensure adequate real resource transfers to developing countries. This follows from the primary purpose of the International Monetary Fund as enshrined in Article I(ii): "To facilitate the expansion and balanced growth of international trade, and to contribute thereby to the promotion and maintenance of high levels of employment and real income and to the development of the productive resources of all members as primary objectives of economic policy."

## The Analytical Basis of Surveillance

**78.** The process of surveillance for international adjustment should focus on international policy interactions and economic linkages among the major industrial countries which are mainly responsible for the course of the world economy. Multilateral surveillance and bilateral (Article IV) consultations should form two stages of the surveillance process, rather than two parallel operations. The first stage would involve multilateral discussions and negotiations to be conducted on a regular basis within the framework of the IMF about a mutually consistent set of objectives, and a set of policies to collectively achieve these objectives. The aim might be to search for a set of outcomes or "objective indicators" or "targets," that appear to be sustainable in the medium term and desirable to all parties. This should be quite feasible when the multilateral surveillance exercise is limited to a few major industrial countries, such as the key currency countries. The second stage would involve a comparison between the actual outcomes and the recommended targets or indicators, and a discussion of what measures would be appropriate when the two differ. This stage might most efficiently be conducted on a bilateral basis as part of Article IV consultations.

**79.** The form in which multilateral surveillance has so far been conducted is through the annual World Economic Outlook (WEO) type of exercise. Such exercises could serve a useful purpose if they provide a background for multilateral consultations about the mutually consistent set of objectives and policies as mentioned above. The WEO should clearly spell out the international repercussions and interactions of national policies of the major industrial countries and contain fairly specific proposals of policies for these countries. These analyses should be considered by the Fund Board to recommend a set of policies and the likely outcomes or performance indicators. The Fund should prepare follow-up reports on the implementation of the recommended policies, deviations from them, and the actual outcomes. These reports should be thoroughly discussed by the Fund Board.

## Pressures to Make Surveillance Effective

**80.** It is generally accepted that while the Fund's leverage over developing economies has been very large, there is virtually no effective pressure on industrial countries to comply with the Fund's policy advice. For improving effectiveness in surveillance over industrial countries, it will be necessary for the Fund to continuously watch and monitor key economic developments pertaining to these countries and to devise procedures for exercising pressure both during multilateral surveillance and in Article IV consultations.

**81.** Bilateral consultations with the major industrial countries would have to focus on policy evaluation against this multilateral framework of international adjustment. Once an agreement is reached on the policy changes, deviations in implementing the suggested policy changes should give rise to information notices. The country concerned could raise the matter in the Fund's Executive Board for a full discussion as to how and why the suggested policies could not be put into effect.

**82.** If the Board is not convinced of the country's explanations, it could request the Managing Director of the Fund to discuss the matter with the country concerned and report back to the Board the outcome of the discussions for further appropriate action.

**83.** The suggested framework for multilateral surveillance of major industrial countries, and taking it up in detail during the bilateral Article IV consultations, would go a long way toward correcting the current asymmetry in the exercise of the Fund's surveillance function.

**84.** In this context, it is useful and in fact necessary to distinguish the content of Article IV consultations that the Fund should conduct with major industrial countries from that of the consultations that should be had with developing countries. In the case of major industrial countries, the consultations should concentrate on a thorough assessment of their national economic policies, including the exchange rate policies, their domestic and international impact, and also their effect on the adjustment efforts of other countries of the world. The consultations should continue to give, as at present, details of current account developments. Emphasis should also be placed on the developments in the capital account in view of the large mobility of capital in recent years. They should also cover the restrictions placed on the international adjustment mechanism such as trade restrictions and other protectionist measures, market-distorting policies, and structural rigidities.

**85.** The consultation reports of the major industrial countries may contain references to the policy recommendations made by the Fund during the previous consultation and the measures undertaken by the member since then in this regard. For effective surveillance, the Fund may be allowed to make greater use of the supplemental surveillance procedures whenever exchange rate developments or other key developments having an impact on other members or on the functioning of the international monetary system warrant. The procedures outlined in the Executive Board decision in 1979 in this regard could be of guidance in invoking supplemental consultations in between the Article IV consultations.

86. Recommendations of policies for developing country members should be made with a view to promoting adjustment as a part of economic development. The underlying needs of finance for such adjustment should be assessed and methods for providing such finance should be indicated. While making the policy suggestions, the part that exogenous factors play in the adjustment efforts of these countries and also the effects of the actions of other countries, in particular the major industrial countries, should be clearly brought out.

87. In prescribing exchange rate policies for developing countries, it is essential to consider that changes in resource allocation are time consuming and would need adequate financing. Often changes in exchange rates of developing countries would have to be supported by complementary policies. While exchange rate devaluation may be useful for improving competitiveness and external viability in developing countries, it could also, as the experience has shown, stimulate cost inflation, causing economic disruption and negating the intended effects of lowering export prices in terms of foreign currency. It is much less useful in countries that have to rely on exports of traditional agricultural and mineral commodities; and simultaneous efforts by a number of countries to undercut the export prices of competitors have often resulted in losses for all. In many developing countries, controls to limit capital outflows may become necessary for the stability of exchange and interest rates. Flexibility in regard to use of multiple currency practices is also necessary in certain cases.

88. The underlying confidentiality of the exchange of information and discussions between the members and the Fund should be preserved. As such, no publicity should be given to the conclusions of the consultations either through release of a statement or through release of reports.

## Enhanced Surveillance

89. The Fund should continue to play its role in easing the debt burden of developing countries through arrangements for use of Fund resources and also in a catalytic manner for facilitating the flow of resources from banks and other creditors. Deputies expressed concern over the implications of IMF involvement in "enhanced surveillance." It is viewed by the Deputies as yet another piece of evidence of creditor unwillingness to restore normal access to external financing despite significant adjustment efforts. The catalytic role of the IMF should, in principle, be exercised without "enhanced surveillance." However, in cases where it proves necessary "enhanced surveillance" should be considered exceptional and undertaken only at the request of a member country. It is justified only if it secures financing from non-Fund sources in the context of a multiyear debt rescheduling. It is important that in "enhanced surveillance," priority is given to policies aimed at promoting self-sustained growth. However, the Fund's continued analysis and policy advice under "enhanced surveillance" arrangements should be clearly differentiated from the programs under Fund arrangements. The main objective of "enhanced surveillance" should be the early normalization of market relations between the member country and the international financial system. To this end, the period under which the country is under "enhanced surveillance" should be limited to the debt consolidation period or the grace period.

## Chapter VI: Management of International Liquidity and the SDR

### Management of International Liquidity

90. The changeover to a flexible exchange rate system did not bring about any perceptible decline in the world demand for reserves. The reasons for this are well known. Countries, whether they floated or pegged their currencies, continued to need adequate reserves for intervention purposes. The experience with the floating exchange rate system has also not been satisfactory, especially due to large, and at times, violent swings; this, together with large payments disequilibria and high interest rates, contributed to countries' holding substantial reserves to protect themselves against uncertainties. In addition, larger reserves were needed especially by developing countries to insulate themselves against frequent exogenous "shocks," deterioration of terms of trade, protracted recession, and increasing protectionism in industrial countries. Adequate reserves were also needed to prove "creditworthiness" and for access to international markets.

91. The supply of international liquidity was in recent years markedly influenced by credit made available

by international commercial banks. For some developing countries, they provided a fairly substantial source of liquidity. But there was also a large number of developing countries which could not afford the high cost of commercial credit and which continued to rely on the supply of official finance, SDR allocations, and conditional credit for financing their balance of payments needs.

92. Dependency on commercial banks as a source of liquidity brought with it substantial debt-service requirements often too large in relation to receipts from trade. Floating interest rates, together with their volatility in the last four years, increased the variability of interest payments. Bunching of maturities also made it difficult to refinance their debt. And borrowed reserves were in fact withdrawn when they were most needed. Since mid-1982, bank lending sharply declined.

93. Developing countries are now facing a severe shortage of external real resources. A number of countries had to run large trade surpluses to service their debt and to build up minimum reserves required for normal transaction and precautionary purposes. This situation has been exacerbated by the falling commodity prices, which are at the lowest level since 1980. Oil prices as well as prices of certain manufactures exported by developing countries are also on the decline. Low-income countries which have only limited access to commercial borrowing are experiencing an equally severe liquidity problem. Official assistance to them fell in real terms in recent years. Many of these countries had accumulated arrears. They have to approach the Fund for support, but often have to face reduced access limits and tightened conditionality without the provision of adequate liquidity.

94. The conditions of supply of international reserve assets and the availability of liquidity relative to need, including the manner in which their supply is distributed among countries, are more important than the size of world aggregate reserve holdings. The present inadequacy as well as unevenness in international liquidity cannot be corrected or even controlled through market processes. It is often held that access to commercial credit would depend on "creditworthiness," which in turn is dependent upon adjustment. But despite vigorous adjustment policies pursued by developing countries leading to a sizable improvement in their current account position, "creditworthiness" was not restored; nor was there a reversal of the decline in bank lending. Reserves have to be built up first to earn "creditworthiness" and, for obtaining such a position, developing countries will have to either generate current account surpluses or depend upon other nonmarket sources.

95. Improvements in the operation of capital markets, whether through risk evaluation by banks or by increased deregulation, will not automatically improve the liquidity position of developing countries. In fact, the conditions that determine the availability of reserves through the capital markets are similar to the conditions that influence the performance of the borrowing countries or their "creditworthiness." Improvement in reserves on which "creditworthiness" hinges, would take place only when the balance of payments position is strengthened. It is necessary to recognize that movements of exchange rates, inflation rates, and growth of output and trade that affect the balance of payments of these countries are themselves subject to the influence of the domestic policies pursued by major industrial countries. These policies have not been internationally consistent and coordinated and have therefore not promoted international adjustment.

96. The scope for international liquidity policy is, therefore, limited by the willingness of major countries to consider the international impact of their policies and to respond to the urgings made in the representative international fora. The Fund is given the tasks of overseeing the international monetary system and ensuring that members collaborate with the Fund and with other members in pursuit of the objective of "better international surveillance of international liquidity" (Article VIII, Section 7). Therefore, in addition to stricter surveillance over exchange rate and other macroeconomic policies of the major industrial countries, the Fund should be enabled to influence the liquidity needs of the world economy through a more efficient SDR creation and distribution than it has so far been able to do.

## The SDR

97. The Articles of Agreement of the Fund provide for creation of additional liquidity through the allocation of SDRs. The Second Amendment of the Articles of Agreement, which became effective as late as 1978, provides that the members of the Fund should collaborate with the objective of making the SDR "the principal reserve asset" in the international monetary system. The main purposes of the allocation of SDRs are: to meet the growing liquidity needs of the world, to make the supply of international liquidity less dependent on the settlement of balances of a few countries, and to enable nonreserve countries to acquire reserves without having to generate balance of payments surpluses.

98. The SDR has not yet assumed a major role in the international system mainly because of its meager allocation. So far only SDR 21.4 billion has been allocated. This constitutes 5.3 percent of the total nongold reserves. There have been sporadic allocations

in two basic periods but since 1981, in spite of a substantial liquidity shortage, there have been none.

**99.** There is also the need to improve the quality of the SDR as a reserve asset and as an increasingly acceptable unit of account in private transactions. The evolution of a multicurrency reserve system has not reduced the need for an internationally controlled reserve asset such as the SDR. On the contrary, SDRs would provide stability to the international system more effectively than the multicurrency reserves by reducing the effects of volatility of exchange rates. By assuring adequate supplies, the SDR system would obviate the necessity of depending on one or two countries for supply of international liquidity. Besides, the SDR has an important role to play in a system where borrowed reserves are not available for most countries facing severe balance of payments adjustment.

**100.** The ratio of non-gold reserves to imports, which constitutes one of the important indicators for the measurement of demand for reserves, continues to be around 21 percent, much lower than the 28 percent in 1982 and 23 percent in 1978, when the previous allocation in the third basic period was agreed. The modest rise in the non-gold reserves, evidenced recently, was from an extremely low level of 1982, and it occurred basically on account of a substantial accrual of such reserves to a handful of countries; in the case of nearly 30 out of 64 non-oil developing countries for which data are available up to 1984, the level of non-gold reserves was lower than that at the end of 1979. Many of them had reductions in their reserves ranging between 50 and 90 percent. In addition, curtailment of access to financial markets has seriously affected the availability of borrowed resources to many countries. This has compelled developing countries to carry larger reserves. Even among those countries which had increased their reserves, many had accomplished it not by large increases in export earnings, but by a substantial curtailment of imports. Currently, the ratio of non-gold reserves to aggregate trade imbalances is more or less at the same level as in 1980, which was the lowest since 1974. If total reserves including gold valued at market prices are reckoned, their proportions to imports and aggregate trade imbalances would still show declines since 1979. Total reserves of all countries had declined by about 19 percent over this period.

**101.** The recent World Economic Outlook exercise implied a continuing expansion of world trade in SDR terms throughout the remainder of the 1980s. Even if the non-gold reserve holdings were to rise to a level that establishes the average reserve ratio for the period 1973–83 (21.5 percent), they would have to grow at an annual rate of about 10 percent per annum until 1990 (or in six years), implying an increase of about SDR 300 billion. According to this calculation, the proposal contained in the 1984 Group of Twenty-Four Revised Program of an annual allocation of SDR 15 billion would be much lower than what is warranted by the long-term global need of liquidity.

**102.** One fear that has often been expressed is that SDR allocations would increase the stock of world reserves and fuel inflation. This fear, however, is not well founded. The supply of reserves is demand determined and the SDR is a substitute for other forms of reserves. The total reserve stocks do not rise in the long run as a result of additional allocations. The first round effect of an allocation may be increased spending by liquidity-constrained countries. But considering their magnitudes, it is far fetched to suppose that SDR allocations, even on a scale sufficient to satisfy the reserve accumulation needs of developing countries, would create excess demand and stimulate inflation in industrial countries. On the contrary, industrial countries should welcome a consequential increase in export demand from the developing countries, which would reduce the pressures created by their need to accommodate the improvement in the current account balance of the developing countries. The spillover effects of an SDR allocation on industrial countries would thus be positive.

**103.** The objective of making the SDR the principal reserve asset in the international monetary system, as expressed in Article VIII, Section 7, has not been promoted. On the contrary, SDRs constitute a smaller proportion of total reserves now than they did in 1976. Private use of the SDR too has languished. The motive for the original commitment to make the SDR the principal reserve asset was a desire to construct as symmetrical a system as possible, so as to avoid the tensions, instability, and inequity of arrangements in which one or a few countries supply reserve currencies and all other countries have to earn or borrow their reserves. There is no good reason for abandoning this objective, especially when the multiple currency reserve system has contributed to serious volatility and misalignment of exchange rates of major currencies.

**104.** To make the SDR the principal reserve asset as required under the Articles, SDRs should be issued on a regular annual basis with a view to ensuring that their proportion in reserves rises progressively. Such allocations would permit pursuit of adjustment policies without too much additional austerity in a number of developing countries and help stimulate demand for exports of developed countries.

**105.** Countries which do not have access to international financial markets are dependent on other sources of finance for acquisition of reserves in the absence of SDR allocations. Concessional financing could be a substitute for additional SDR allocation. But only limited sums of mildly concessional financing are at present available and that, too, on highly conditional terms. This source of financing is too inadequate to meet the reserve needs of these countries or even to promote "creditworthiness" to increase their access to capital markets. Only an unconditional SDR allocation could provide the required reserves strength for most of these countries. As the 1984 Group of Twenty-Four Revised Program has stressed, the unconditional use of SDRs must remain inviolate.

106. The circumstances governing the supply of liquidity differ sharply as between different groups of Fund members. Industrial countries have an interest in acquiring adequate reserves and their liquidity needs have been largely met by capital flows. With the withdrawal of commercial bank lending to developing countries, and if official finance is not raised substantially, the only way to meet the liquidity requirements of developing countries is by an adequate allocation of SDRs. In this context, a link between allocation of SDRs and development would not only meet the unfulfilled absorptive capacity of developing countries but also reduce the pressures on the industrial countries to accommodate an improvement in the current account balances of developing countries. While allocations to industrial countries do not augment their liquidity, those to developing countries would offer benefits to all members of the world community. It is, therefore, difficult to see any reason for not adopting the link.

## Chapter VII: Role of the IMF

107. The purposes of the International Monetary Fund were set out in Article I of the Articles of Agreement, which remained much the same even after the two amendments to the Articles. The role of the Fund was to change depending on the changes in the international monetary and financial system so as to achieve those purposes.

108. During the past forty years, the Fund certainly played an important role in the pursuit of some of these purposes. But it was not very successful in fulfilling the aspirations of a large number of developing countries, which today hold over a third of the Fund's voting power and an overwhelming majority of the Fund's membership. Developments in the international economy in the late seventies and early eighties affected most countries adversely, and developing countries found to their cost that they were more vulnerable than others. As pointed out in the 1984 Group of Twenty-Four Revised Program, "the conventional response to the international monetary disarray has been to find ad hoc solutions. The result has been that we have lived from one crisis to another."

109. The International Monetary Fund is expected to play a central role in the operation of the international monetary system. It provides a forum for consultation and cooperation in international monetary relations, but in many respects it falls far short of needs. Its surveillance so far has not ensured that the policies of major members are consistent with the requirements of international economic growth and financial stability; it has not been able to supplement adequately the stock of international reserves through SDR allocations and promote the SDR as the principal reserve asset as required under the Articles; while it tried to smooth the process of adjustment of international payments, with some success, its concept of adjustment has not always been found appropriate.

110. The previous chapters dealt with the Fund's role in surveillance over member governments' policies, and in the provision of international liquidity. This chapter discusses the Fund's role in promoting balance of payments adjustments, the provision of required finance, its resource base, and related issues.

111. When discussing payments imbalances, it is conventional to distinguish between transitory imbalances, which should be financed, and persistent imbalances, which require both finance and adjustment. The Fund has a role to play in both of them.

## Transitory Balance of Payments Problems

112. Transitory payments problems are met by international reserves, borrowing from capital markets, or drawing on Fund facilities. Because of the liquidity squeeze to which developing countries have been subjected, and their difficulty in borrowing from international capital markets, the Fund's facilities have for some years been used much more by developing than by industrial countries.

113. The compensatory financing facility (CFF) was the Fund's first attempt to relate the provision of its low-conditionality finance to the events outside the control of the borrowing country that produce export fluctuations and, thereby, a payments deficit which could be assumed to be transitory. It has been extensively used by developing countries, especially since the liberalization of access in 1976.

114. In 1981, compensatory finance was extended to cover increased costs of cereal imports as well as shortfalls in the value of export receipts. Instead of extending the principle of low-conditionality finance for deficits due to factors beyond the control of the members, the Fund has since 1983 proceeded to emasculate one of its most successful operations, by

making access under the CFF highly conditional. The access limits were also reduced from 100 percent to 83 percent of quota. These were retrograde steps imposed at a time when developing countries were exceptionally short of liquidity.

**115.** The high conditionality in the CFF should be reversed and the access should be restored to 100 percent of quota, in order to diminish the vulnerability of developing countries to exogenous shocks. The CFF should be extended to cover not only the export shortfalls but also a deterioration in terms of trade that is quantifiable. Further, CFF drawings should be related to calculated shortfalls rather than to quotas. The CFF should compensate the full amount of the calculated shortfall, and should be offered on a virtually automatic basis. As recessions have tended to become deeper and the cycles longer in the recent past, the balance of payments stress on most developing countries has increased and therefore the repayment period of the CFF should be extended.

**116.** Large variability in interest rates in recent years had a severe impact on indebted developing countries. Therefore, a new facility to provide financing for interest rate increases needs to be introduced. Moreover, there is a strong case for creating a comprehensive CFF to provide low-conditionality finance to cover deficits resulting from any exogenous factor that can be presumed to be temporary. It would help countries to manage their economies rationally and to provide a countercyclical influence on the world economy. Different facilities, such as those relating to export earnings, cost of cereal imports, increase in interest rates, commodity specific export shortfalls as proposed by UNCTAD (United Nations Conference on Trade Development) or practiced by STABEX, could all be components of such a comprehensive facility.

## Persistent Imbalances Requiring Adjustment

**117.** In contrast to transitory payments imbalances, deficits that threaten to be persistent require both large scale finance and adjustment. The Fund is enjoined by its Articles to promote adjustment without members resorting to measures destructive of national or international prosperity (Article I(v)). This requires that adjustment measures not invariably lead to lowering of economic growth and development in the deficit countries. Correction of deficits through deflationary measures should be considered only as a last resort.

**118.** Clearly, policies should be devised according to the nature of the underlying disequilibrium. If payments disequilibria arise from excess domestic demand, more restrained fiscal and monetary policies will be in order. If they arise from exchange rate misalignment, the appropriate remedy lies in correcting the exchange rate. In either case, the policies should try to minimize their adverse impact on the growth of real output and income distribution. However, in most cases, persistent payments disequilibria in developing countries are structural. Because of low short-run elasticities of substitution, a country producing raw materials will not be able to switch resources quickly into alternatives needed to restore equilibrium. External balance can then be achieved by lowering domestic demand, implying idle resources; but the preferred course would be structural adjustment which raises the economy's capacity to produce tradables. When improvement of the trade balance requires a supply response, either through increasing productivity or provision of specific inputs and technology or expansion of capacity, demand restraint is rarely sufficient, and often not even a part of the appropriate response to a balance of payments disequilibrium.

**119.** Recognition of the need in many cases for supply response or structural adjustment contributed to the development of multiyear adjustment programs, and specifically to the creation of the EFF. However, the design of some of these programs has not always focused on promoting the necessary shifts of productive resources within the context of policies for investment and economic growth. Nor do they take into account the adverse consequences for income distribution or inflation in the short run.

**120.** Reorientation of conditionality criteria from demand deflation to growth-oriented structural adjustment implies a need to lengthen program periods and to increase the level of financing. In fact, it may at times be appropriate to finance a transitory deterioration in the payments balance, if imported raw materials and investment goods are needed to reactivate or expand capacity in the tradables sector. Moreover, longer programs provide an opportunity to ensure that the needed structural reforms are undertaken. There is the danger in a short-term stabilization effort that a transitory recovery of the balance of payments will be achieved through demand deflation, while necessary structural adjustments are neglected.

**121.** In the past two years there has been a considerable underplaying of the EFF, with more and more of the programs supported by the Fund being stand-by arrangements. This development could contribute to unnecessary economic destabilization in many developing countries. In fact, excepting in cases where imbalances to be corrected are of a comparatively mild nature, the EFF should be used extensively.

**122.** It is recognized that the balance of payments problems of most low-income countries are structural in nature, caused mainly by persistent deterioration in their terms of trade, their disproportionately large debt service burden, their decline in the flow of ODA, and their very limited capability to attract external resources from nonofficial sources. These problems have been seriously compounded by devastating droughts of unprecedented proportions that have hit many African countries. Of late, the majority of low-income countries have experienced net outflows of resources, including to the multilateral financial institutions. In view of the particularly difficult structural problems of these countries, it is essential that the Fund provide larger and longer-term financing in support of their structural adjustment programs than has been provided so far.

123. Some Fund programs have broken down in recent years because of excessively rigid performance criteria, which were not revised in the light of unforeseen developments beyond the control of the borrowing country. There is a need for greater flexibility in the application of such criteria. The Fund's operations are dependent on the revolving character of its resources, and it is necessary that repayment obligations to the Fund are settled on time. In cases where the balance of payments situation, made adverse by exogenous factors, makes it practically impossible for a country to repay according to a fixed schedule, mechanical application of sanctions available under the Articles of Agreement would be self-defeating and would not serve the purpose for which the loan to the country concerned was made. It may be necessary for the Fund to be more flexible in the application of Article V, Section 7(g), which provides for postponement of obligations "because discharge on the due date would result in exceptional hardship for the member." However, to help these countries become current in their obligations to the Fund, new mechanisms should be evolved, in collaboration with the World Bank and regional development institutions, to provide longer-term assistance for orderly adjustment of these countries.

## Need for Concessionality in IMF Lending

124. It is recognized internationally that there is a need to provide finance at concessional rates to developing countries, especially the low-income countries. However, the burden of costs of Fund resources has fallen disproportionately on the borrowing countries in recent years. On account of inadequacy of Fund quotas, the Fund resorted to borrowing to supplement its own resources and, increasingly, to provide financing to borrowing members by using a mix of borrowed and quota resources, and passed on the cost of borrowed resources fully to borrowing members. Besides, due to the steep increases in the rate of charge to borrowers, the borrowing costs of developing countries have greatly increased in the recent years. The grant element in the rate of charge fell steeply from about 30 percent during 1980–82 to negligible levels currently.

125. While interest rates in international markets have been declining, Fund charges on the use of quota resources have been raised during the last two years. By discouraging low-income members from borrowing from the Fund at reasonable cost, the Fund's capacity to promote orderly adjustment has been undermined. It is therefore important to establish facilities and mechanisms within the Fund, such as an interest subsidy account, on a stable basis to ameliorate the situation. Moreover, in view of the extremely difficult situation in which many developing countries are placed, it is necessary to revive the Trust Fund and to make concessional loans to eligible countries.

## The Volume of IMF Resources

126. Because of the special role that the IMF is expected to play in the international adjustment process, quotas must remain the primary source of the Fund's financial resources. However, the IMF quotas had, in the aggregate, formed only about 5 percent of total imports at the end of 1984, as against 12 percent in the sixties.

127. The ratios of Fund quotas to world trade and to current account deficits are useful indicators of the shortage of Fund resources. Both these ratios have been declining sharply. While non-gold reserves and international bank lending rose some six- or sevenfold between 1970 and 1982, the size of the IMF, as measured by the sum of the quotas, the borrowing arrangements, and the SDR allocations, increased only threefold and the quotas barely doubled. However measured, the quantitative contribution of the IMF to balance of payments financing and to world reserves has declined sharply both in relation to need and in relation to other sources.

128. During the Eighth General Review of Quotas, the majority of the Fund membership favored a doubling of the Fund quotas as being essential to enable the Fund to discharge its responsibilities. This recommendation did not take into account the increase needed due to the impact of the pressures on the balance of payments of the debtor countries from mid-1982 onwards and the withdrawal of new lending by commercial banks. The increase in quotas that was eventually adopted amounted to only 47.5 percent. Despite the inadequacy of the quota increase, normal annual access limits were reduced in stages from 150 percent to 95–102 percent of quota, from 450 percent to 280–395 percent, over three-year periods, and from 600 percent to 408 percent cumulatively. Higher limits were to be

considered only in exceptional circumstances. Access limits were also reduced for the CFF from 100 percent to 83 percent of quota.

129. As a result, the adjustment programs undertaken by developing countries could not be financed adequately and had more stringent conditionality than was appropriate for the structural changes that their situations warranted. The inadequacy of resources stood in the way of the Fund playing its due role in financing and adjustment.

130. There is, therefore, the need for a substantial increase of quotas under the Ninth General Review, which should be advanced. In order to avoid the political and procedural difficulties of negotiating quota increases, it may be desirable to tie quotas to some appropriate measure of the size of the world economy. In the absence of such an automatic link, the normal interval between quota reviews should be reduced to three years.

131. Pending the Ninth General Review, it will be necessary for the Fund to supplement its resources adequately by resorting to borrowing, preferably from official sources, so that real access to Fund resources is not reduced in these difficult times. Until such time as the size of quotas bears an appropriate relationship to some appropriate measure of the size of the world economy, it is imperative to maintain the policy of enlarged access without dilution.

## Enlarged Access Policy and Access Limits

132. The enlarged access policy of the Fund, introduced in 1981, has been a useful instrument in making finances available to a number of countries that were affected by large payments imbalances. Developing countries consider that despite some improvement in the world economy in the last two years, recovery has been weak, fragile, and uneven. The outlook for 1985 at present is, in fact, bleak. A large number of developing countries continue to experience serious balance of payments difficulties. There is no reason to believe that their requirements of financing will fall to permit a reversal of the policy of enlarged access. Indeed, they consider that the present access limits, are, as a result of the recent reductions, too meager and should be enhanced.

133. Developing countries consider that the policy of enlarged access cannot be dealt with appropriately except in conjunction with the question of adequacy of quotas. Until an appropriate relationship is re-established between Fund quotas and size of the world economy, access limits should be enhanced.

134. The fact that the drawings on the Fund in 1984 were lower than in 1983 by no means implies that there was any reduction in the size of the members' needs. One of the main reasons for the shortfall is the increasing difficulties faced by the member countries in meeting high conditionality and performance criteria of growing complexity, leading to suspension of many programs. In addition, the semiautomaticity of the CFF was replaced by reduced access and high conditionality. There was also a noticeable shift towards reduction in actual access in determining the amount of finance provided under Fund programs. Given the severe compression of imports in many countries in the past few years, output growth rates, imports, and the aggregate current account deficits would have been higher had there been additional external financing consistent with the countries' longer-term debt-servicing capacity on suitable terms.

135. The external account prospects of developing countries will be subject to great uncertainties in the coming years. For many of the countries that have had adjustment programs with the Fund, continued Fund support will remain essential for their progress towards balance of payments viability. In addition to large interest repayments, the highly indebted countries face a large hump in debt servicing over the coming years which would require substantial financing. Even to mobilize funds from commercial banks, Fund financing may have to play a catalytic role.

136. Considering the continuing and serious strain on the international monetary system, heavy debt-service burdens on developing countries that are expected to become accentuated in the next few years, and the inadequacy of Fund resources to meet the requirements of members facing balance of payments difficulties, it is important that the criteria for activating the GAB be relaxed. The GAB and other similar arrangements, however, are not a substitute for adequate growth in quota resources.

## IMF/IBRD Collaboration

137. Developing countries consider that coordination between the IMF and the World Bank should not lead to cross conditionality but should help further their mutual objectives of providing resources to developing countries. Closer contacts between the managements and staffs of the two institutions could help foster understanding of each other's points of view. However, it would not be advisable to seek some kind of uniformity of advice. Such a step would be counterproductive, could lead to cross conditionality, would dilute the respective responsibilities of the two institutions, and could become a means of exerting a concerted pressure on borrowing developing countries. Any policy advice by these institutions would therefore have to be in keeping with their respective roles. If there were to be a coordination of policy advice on a

country, it would be essential to obtain the country's consent in this process.

**138.** As far as the World Bank is concerned, its primary role should continue to be one of commitment to development, growth, and poverty alleviation, as enshrined in its Articles of Agreement. Developing countries consider that there should not be an undue emphasis on conditional lending or increasing conditionality linked to the quantum of lending. The World Bank should play a role in supporting debtor countries so that adjustment in these countries takes place in an environment of growth. The Bank should take effective steps quickly to negotiate a General Capital Increase so as to enable its lending to be expanded sufficiently to fully meet the needs of developing countries. In this context, developing countries are concerned that the net transfers from the World Bank to them are projected to decline over the medium term and to turn negative by the end of the decade, a development which needs to be avoided by an institution whose main purpose is to transfer resources to developing countries to promote economic growth.

## The Decision-Making Process

**139.** The 1984 Group of Twenty-Four Revised Program has made the following recommendations on the decision-making process in the international financial institutions, which the Deputies wish to reiterate:

> The role of developing countries in the decision-making process in the international financial institutions needs to be substantially increased. The system of weighted voting has led to a situation where, after the Eighth Quota Review, developing countries as a group have no more than 38 percent of total votes. While the principle of weighted voting may be unavoidable in financial institutions, a better balance in the voting pattern is needed for a more equitable and effective functioning of these institutions.

> The share of developing countries in the total votes in the multilateral financial institutions should be increased to 50 percent. For this purpose, consideration might be given to, inter alia, an increase in basic votes. The present geographical representation of developing country regions in the Boards of the Bank and the Fund should be preserved.

## Chapter VIII: The Debt Problem and Transfer of Resources

### Problems Relating to External Debt

**140.** External indebtedness of developing countries increased substantially during the seventies. This increase had four characteristics: first, private bank lending became the single most important channel for the transfer of resources from surplus to deficit countries; second, the conditions on which these credits were provided were harder and the maturities shorter than development financing provided by international development finance institutions; third, the bulk of debt was largely accounted for by a relatively small number of countries; and finally, bank financing flows and the conditions on which these were provided showed a procyclical pattern, tending to increase on softer terms when export commodity prices were favorable and to retrench and harden when export earnings declined.

**141.** As a result of these factors, by the beginning of the eighties the external debt situation of the developing countries had registered an overall deterioration in its average term structure, adding a huge servicing burden and a significant element of instability to the international monetary system. By the middle of 1982 a number of exogenous factors, which were described in the earlier chapters, combined to produce the debt crisis. Their effect was compounded by significant shortcomings in the policies of many debtor countries. Tightening of regulations by bank supervisory authorities may also have had an impact on the availability of bank finance. A crisis of confidence had developed regarding the ability of some major borrowers to meet their external commitments. It affected not only these countries but also other borrowers as well as the commercial lending institutions.

**142.** The combination of a decline in capital inflows with continuing high interest rates has resulted in massive negative resource transfers from the developing countries. For Latin America as a whole, debt-service payments to banks are estimated to have amounted to $30 billion in 1983 and $27 billion in 1984, requiring large trade surpluses to be generated.

**143.** Debtor countries have undertaken strenuous adjustment efforts in response to the external environment. The consequential adjustment process is having strong social and political consequences for many debtor countries, including a serious decline in their standards of living and a deterioration in their social fabric. In spite of their harsh adjustment efforts, external debt servicing continues to impose a very heavy burden. The situation requires imaginative solutions involving debt restructuring over the long term, and there is an urgent need to move towards a "positive" type of adjustment, consistent with sustained growth of output in the medium and the long run.

**144.** Capital flight has been an especially acute problem for several of these countries in recent years, accounting for a sizable proportion of their accumulated debt. It is recognized that unstable conditions in debtor countries have on occasion triggered such capital flows. But in order to ensure financial stability, developed countries should, through their regulatory agencies, support the efforts of the authorities of developing countries to discourage capital outflows from those developing countries which are facing acute capital flight problems.

**145.** Multiyear restructuring of bank debts has been a helpful development since it prevented a bunching of maturities. However, it does not by itself solve the debt problem, since, after restructuring, debtor developing countries are left with a major resource transfer problem due to debt-servicing requirements, a result with severe adverse effects on their economies. Moreover, this outcome also poses serious questions on the stability of the international monetary system. In this connection, urgent consideration may have to be given to evolving mechanisms that would roll over or refinance a certain proportion of interest payments, i.e., those above the long-term trend real rate of interest.

**146.** A question arises whether in the event of continuing or increasing reverse transfers (and they will increase as long as the rate of growth of net lending is less than the rate of interest), sufficient resources for expanding investment in export capacity will be available to these countries. If exports do not increase sufficiently, debt-service difficulties could increase over time. More broadly, the issue is whether heavily indebted countries can combine the attainment of satisfactory rates of growth with meeting debt-service payments in full. Several elements will have a bearing on the solution of this issue in a satisfactory manner. Among these are (a) the future rate of growth of the major industrial countries; (b) the international level of interest rates and the dollar rates; (c) the access of developing countries' exports to industrial country markets and the expansion of world trade; (d) the flow of resources to developing countries from financial intermediaries, including international financial institutions; and (e) sustained adjustment efforts on the part of debtor countries over the medium term, coupled with reallocation of resources in favor of exports.

**147.** There are, however, considerable uncertainties regarding the manner in which each of these elements would develop. In fact, it would be easy to envisage circumstances in which the unfavorable evolution of one or more of these factors would have a cumulative adverse impact on the others. Thus, a slowdown in the world economy, higher rates of interest, and growing protectionism could add considerably to the heavy debt-service burden, posing the risk that for at least some debtors the situation would become unsustainable. Without clear signs of economic progress the governments of debtor countries would be faced with political and social pressures making it difficult for them to reconcile the objectives of restoring growth in their countries with the prospective payments of debt service.

**148.** Since the debt crisis may be seen as a result of excessive lending by the commercial banks, abrupt policy changes, and, in some cases, an unbalanced policy mix by industrial countries leading to historically high interest rates, and inadequate policies by many debtor countries, as well as realistic formulae and viable mechanisms for its solution need to be found. The problem requires the cooperation of debtor and industrial countries, commercial banks, and international financial institutions in the discharge of their respective responsibilities; also required is the co-responsibility of debtors and creditors, symmetry of adjustment, and cooperative efforts aimed at a durable solution to the debt problem in a global framework.

**149.** Present problems have arisen to a considerable extent due to the absence of adequate sources of development finance, which led many developing countries to resort to short- and medium-term financing from international capital markets. The sources of finance from capital markets are bound to be greatly reduced in the future. Besides, the earlier pattern of recycling, which had a destabilizing influence on the international monetary system, has generated serious doubts as to the adequacy of the role of commercial lending in the system. The lesson learned from recent experience is that heavy reliance on medium- and short-term borrowing for development financing is bound to give rise to liquidity problems in the medium term, even if such financing were directed to sound and viable projects. Consequently, there is a need to design new financing mechanisms for orderly resource transfer to developing countries, and, in this context, the need to expand the resource base of existing financial institutions such as the World Bank, the regional development banks, and the IMF becomes all the more imperative to enable them to play a much larger role in the recycling process in the years to come.

## Trade and Finance

**150.** In recognition of the interdependence of money, finance, and trade in the global economy, it is important to emphasize the close relationship between expanding world trade and the solution of balance of payments problems, including the indebtedness of developing countries. Developed countries should therefore roll back protectionist measures, refrain from introducing new restrictions, and improve access for exports of developing countries to their markets.

## Transfer of Resources to Developing Countries

151. The recent record regarding the transfer of real resources to developing countries has been disappointing. The transfer of resources from official sources has not even made up, in recent years, for the unprecedented losses incurred by developing countries on account of the adverse movements in their terms of trade and high interest rates. The quality and composition of aid have also witnessed a considerable deterioration.

152. In the low-income countries, slow growth does most to perpetuate and accentuate poverty. Most human development and poverty alleviation programs have long gestation lags and their output is not directly tradable and often is not even marketable. Commercial financing of such investment is unrealistic. The decline in official aid to low-income countries has resulted in underutilization of capacities, a slowdown of priority investments, and disruption of development projects.

153. Within the framework of official development assistance, the International Development Association (IDA) constitutes a major source of concessional assistance to developing countries, and has played a crucial role in the development of low-income countries through high net transfers, proven effective utilization of resources, alleviation of poverty, and provision of technical assistance. Resources made available to IDA through successive replenishments should represent a substantial increase in real terms. It is of vital importance to maintain the integrity of IDA and avoid the repetition of the regrettable experience of IDA VI and IDA VII. During the mid-term review to be conducted shortly by IDA, additional resources should be made available to restore the IDA VII Replenishment to US$12 billion. It is essential that funding for IDA VIII be substantially larger than that for IDA VI, and efforts should be made to restore the historical rates of growth in IDA. The negotiations for IDA VIII should be started at an early date.

154. There is an urgent need to accelerate the flow of concessional aid to developing countries. Developed countries which have not yet reached the internationally agreed target of 0.7 percent of GNP as official development assistance should, as agreed at UNCTAD VI, redouble their efforts to achieve that target as early as possible and in any case not later than in the second half of the decade. Each developed donor country should establish its program and make a binding commitment for the annual growth rate of official development assistance disbursements. This should result in a general increase in real terms and an improvement in the quality of official development assistance flows to developing countries. It should include program and quick-disbursing aid tailored to development and short-term requirements at macro and sectoral levels, respectively. It should increasingly cover local and recurrent costs; be untied to the maximum extent possible; and be provided on an assured, continuous, and predictable basis. In respect of low-income countries, Resolution 165 (S-IX) of the Trade and Development Board of UNCTAD, relating to the adjustment of terms of past bilateral official assistance so as to improve the net flows in appropriate forms and on highly concessional terms, should be implemented fully and expeditiously.

155. There is an equally urgent need to augment the flow of resources from multilateral development institutions. It is disquieting that at currently projected commitment levels of multilateral development institutions, and particularly the IBRD, both net disbursements and net transfers show a significant decline even in nominal terms. It is estimated that IBRD commitment levels would have to increase at an annual rate of at least 6.2 percent in real terms over the levels reached in FY 1983 if net disbursements and net transfers are to remain relatively steady. This would call for an increase of the capital base of the IBRD. It is essential to take immediate steps to negotiate a General Capital Increase of adequate size to permit the IBRD to expand its lending. Similarly, there is need to increase the capital base of the regional development institutions to ensure that their commitments increase at a satisfactory rate. In this context, it is imperative that donor countries channel a greater proportion of their development assistance through multilateral institutions and reaffirm their commitments to multilateralism.

156. Structural adjustment lending which is quick disbursing should be made less conditional to improve its usefulness to borrowing countries. There is need for an increase in program lending of multilateral financial institutions to at least 25 percent of total loans. The lending programs of these institutions should also become increasingly responsive to the overall priorities, and in particular to sectoral priorities, of the recipient developing countries.

157. The early implementation of the recommendations of the United Nations Conference on the Least Developed Countries held in Paris in September 1981 would go a long way towards relieving the plight of these countries. In particular, donor countries should attain, by 1985 or as soon as possible thereafter, the objective of 0.15 percent of their GNP as ODA for these countries within the overall target of 0.7 percent.

158. Sub-Saharan African countries have been facing particularly acute and persistent problems. The Special Assistance Facility established for sub-Saharan Africa is inadequate, and it is necessary to substantially increase the level and quality of its funding. And the program to tackle the problems of these countries must be urgently implemented.

# Appendix III
# Executive Board Decisions on Surveillance Over Exchange Rate Policies

**1977 Decision and Document**

1. The Executive Board has discussed the implementation of Article IV of the proposed Second Amendment of the Articles of Agreement and has approved the attached document entitled "Surveillance Over Exchange Rate Policies." The Fund shall act in accordance with this document when the Second Amendment becomes effective. In the period before that date the Fund shall continue to conduct consultations in accordance with present procedures and decisions.

2. The Fund shall review the document entitled "Surveillance Over Exchange Rate Policies" at intervals of two years and at such other times as consideration of it is placed on the agenda of the Executive Board.

Decision No. 5392–(77/63)
April 29, 1977

Surveillance Over Exchange Rate Policies

General Principles

Article IV, Section 3(a) provides that "The Fund shall oversee the international monetary system in order to ensure its effective operation, and shall oversee the compliance of each member with its obligations under Section 1 of this Article." Article IV, Section 3(b) provides that in order to fulfill its functions under 3(a), "the Fund shall exercise firm surveillance over the exchange rate policies of members, and shall adopt specific principles for the guidance of all members with respect to those policies." Article IV, Section 3(b) also provides that "The principles adopted by the Fund shall be consistent with cooperative arrangements by which members maintain the value of their currencies in relation to the value of the currency or currencies of other members, as well as with other exchange arrangements of a member's choice consistent with the purposes of the Fund and Section 1 of this Article. These principles shall respect the domestic social and political policies of members, and in applying these principles the Fund shall pay due regard to the circumstances of members." In addition, Article IV, Section 3(b) requires that "Each member shall provide the Fund with the information necessary for such surveillance, and when requested by the Fund, shall consult with it on the member's exchange rate policies."

The principles and procedures set out below, which apply to all members whatever their exchange arrangements and whatever their balance of payments position, are adopted by the Fund in order to perform its functions under Section 3(b). They are not necessarily comprehensive and are subject to reconsideration in the light of experience. They do not deal directly with the Fund's responsibilities referred to in Section 3(a), although it is recognized that there is a close relationship between domestic and international economic policies. This relationship is emphasized in Article IV which includes the following provision: "Recognizing . . . that a principal objective [of the international monetary system] is the continuing development of the orderly underlying conditions that are necessary for financial and economic stability, each member undertakes to collaborate with the Fund and other members to assure orderly exchange arrangements and to promote a stable system of exchange rates."

Principles for the Guidance of Member's Exchange Rate Policies

A. A member shall avoid manipulating exchange rates or the international monetary system in order to prevent effective balance of payments adjustment or to gain an unfair competitive advantage over other members.

B. A member should intervene in the exchange market if necessary to counter disorderly conditions which may be characterized inter alia by disruptive short-term movements in the exchange value of its currency.

C. Members should take into account in their intervention policies the interests of other members including those of the countries in whose currencies they intervene.

Principles of Fund Surveillance over Exchange Rate Policies

1. The surveillance of exchange rate policies shall

be adapted to the needs of international adjustment as they develop. The functioning of the international adjustment process shall be kept under review by the Executive Board and Interim Committee and the assessment of its operation shall be taken into account in the implementation of the principles set forth below.

2. In its surveillance of the observance by members of the principles set forth above, the Fund shall consider the following developments as among those which might indicate the need for discussion with a member:

(i) protracted large-scale intervention in one direction in the exchange market;

(ii) an unsustainable level of official or quasi-official borrowing, or excessive and prolonged short-term official or quasi-official lending, for balance of payments purposes;

(iii) (a) the introduction, substantial intensification, or prolonged maintenance, for balance of payments purposes, of restrictions on, or incentives for, current transactions or payments, or

(b) the introduction or substantial modification for balance of payments purposes of restrictions on, or incentives for, the inflow or outflow of capital;

(iv) the pursuit, for balance of payments purposes, of monetary and other domestic financial policies that provide abnormal encouragement or discouragement to capital flows; and

(v) behavior of the exchange rate that appears to be unrelated to underlying economic and financial conditions including factors affecting competitiveness and long-term capital movements.

3. The Fund's appraisal of a member's exchange rate policies shall be based on an evaluation of the developments in the member's balance of payments against the background of its reserve position and its external indebtedness. This appraisal shall be made within the framework of a comprehensive analysis of the general economic situation and economic policy strategy of the member, and shall recognize that domestic as well as external policies can contribute to timely adjustment of the balance of payments. The appraisal shall take into account the extent to which the policies of the member, including its exchange rate policies, serve the objectives of the continuing development of the orderly underlying conditions that are necessary for financial stability, the promotion of sustained sound economic growth and reasonable levels of employment.

Procedures for Surveillance

I. Each member shall notify the Fund in appropriate detail within thirty days after the Second Amendment becomes effective of the exchange arrangements it intends to apply in fulfillment of its obligations under Article IV, Section 1. Each member shall also notify the Fund promptly of any changes in exchange arrangements.

II. Members shall consult with the Fund regularly under Article IV. The consultations under Article IV shall comprehend the regular consultations under Articles VIII and XIV. In principle such consultations shall take place annually, and shall include consideration of the observance by members of the principles set forth above as well as of a member's obligations under Article IV, Section 1. Not later than three months after the termination of discussions between the member and the staff, the Executive Board shall reach conclusions and thereby complete the consultation under Article IV.

III. Broad developments in exchange rates will be reviewed periodically by the Executive Board, inter alia in discussions of the international adjustment process within the framework of the World Economic Outlook. The Fund will continue to conduct special consultations in preparing for these discussions.

IV. The Managing Director shall maintain close contact with members in connection with their exchange arrangements and exchange policies, and will be prepared to discuss on the initiative of a member important changes that it contemplates in its exchange arrangements or its exchange rate policies.

V. If, in the interval between Article IV consultations, the Managing Director, taking into account any views that may have been expressed by other members, considers that a member's exchange rate policies may not be in accord with the exchange rate principles, he shall raise the matter informally and confidentially with the member, and shall conclude promptly whether there is a question of the observance of the principles. If he concludes that there is such a question, he shall initiate and conduct on a confidential basis a discussion with the member under Article IV, Section 3(b). As soon as possible after the completion of such a discussion, and in any event not later than four months after its initiation, the Managing Director shall report to the Executive Board on the results of the discussion. If, however, the Managing Director is satisfied that the principles are being observed, he shall informally advise all Executive Directors, and the staff shall report on the discussion in the context of the next Article IV consultation; but the Managing Director shall not place the matter on the agenda of the Executive Board unless the member requests that this procedure be followed.

VI. The Executive Directors shall review annually the general implementation of the Fund's surveillance over members' exchange rate policies.

## 1979 Decision

Surveillance: Procedures

. . . .

3. Supplemental surveillance procedure. . . . Whenever the Managing Director considers that a modification in a member's exchange arrangements or exchange rate policies or the behavior of the exchange rate of its currency may be important or may have important effects on other members, whatever the member's exchange arrangement may be, he shall initiate informally and confidentially a discussion with the member before the next regular discussion under Article IV. If he considers after this prior discussion that the matter is of importance, he shall initiate and conduct an ad hoc consultation with the member and shall report to the Executive Board, or informally advise the Executive Directors, on the consultation as promptly as the circumstances permit after conclusion of the consultation. This procedure will supplement the proceedings in Executive Board Decision No. 5392-(77/63), adopted April 29, 1977.

Decision No. 6026-(79/13)
January 22, 1979

# References

Bergsten, C. Fred and John Williamson, "Exchange Rates and Trade Policy," in *Trade Policy in the 1980s*, edited by William R. Cline (Washington: Institute for International Economics, 1983).

Bergstrand, Jeffrey, "Is Exchange Rate Volatility 'Excessive'?" *New England Economic Review* (Boston, September/October 1983), pp. 5–14.

Black, Stanley W., "Central Bank Intervention and the Stability of Exchange Rates," Institute for International Economic Studies Seminar Papers No. 136 (University of Stockholm, February 1980).

Bond, Marian E. and Adalbert Knobl, "Some Implications of North Sea Oil for the U.K. Economy," *Staff Papers*, International Monetary Fund (Washington), Vol. 29 (September 1982), pp. 363–97.

Deppler, Michael and Duncan M. Ripley, "The World Trade Model: Merchandise Trade," *Staff Papers*, International Monetary Fund (Washington), Vol. 25 (March 1978), pp. 147–206.

Dunn, Robert, "Exchange Rate Rigidity, Investment Distortions, and the Failure of Bretton Woods," *Essays in International Finance No. 97*, (Princeton, New Jersey: Princeton University Press, 1973).

Frenkel, Jacob A. and Morris Goldstein, "A Guide to Target Zones," *Staff Papers*, International Monetary Fund (Washington), Vol. 33 (December 1986), forthcoming.

Frenkel, Jacob A. and Michael L. Mussa, "The Efficiency of Foreign Exchange Markets and Measures of Turbulence," *American Economic Review* (Nashville, Tennessee), Vol. 70 (May 1980), pp. 374–81.

Genberg, Hans, "On Choosing the Right Rules for Exchange-Rate Management," *World Economy* (Oxford), Vol. 7 (December 1984), pp. 391–406.

Goldstein Morris and Mohsin Khan, "Income and Price Effects in Foreign Trade," in *Handbook of International Economics*, edited by Ronald W. Jones and Peter B. Kenen (Amsterdam: North-Holland Publishing Co., 1985), Vol. II, pp. 1041–1105.

International Monetary Fund, *The Role of Exchange Rates in the Adjustment of International Payments: A Report by the Executive Directors* (Washington: IMF, 1970).

———, *International Monetary Reform: Documents of the Committee of Twenty* (Washington, IMF, 1974).

———, *Exchange Rate Volatility and World Trade*, a study by the Research Department of the International Monetary Fund, Occasional Paper No. 28 (Washington: IMF, July 1984a).

———, *Issues in the Assessment of the Exchange Rates of Industrial Countries*, a study by the Research Department of the International Monetary Fund, Occasional Paper No. 29 (Washington: IMF, July 1984b).

———, *The Exchange Rate System: Lessons of the Past and Options for the Future*, a study by the Research Department of the International Monetary Fund, Occasional Paper No. 30 (Washington: IMF, July 1984c).

Kenen, Peter B., "Reforming the International Monetary System," paper prepared for presentation to New York Academy of Sciences, September 1985.

Machlup, Fritz, "Comments on 'The Failure of Global Fixity' and 'The Failure of Global Flexibility'," in *EMS: The Emerging European Monetary System*, edited by Robert Triffin (Brussels: National Bank of Belgium, 1979), pp. 65–78.

Makin, John H., *Capital Flows and Exchange-Rate Flexibility in the Post-Bretton Woods Era*, Essays in International Finance No. 103 (Princeton, New Jersey: Princeton University Press, 1974).

Mussa, Michael, "Empirical Regularities in the Behavior of Exchange Rates and Theories of the Foreign Exchange Market," in *Theory, Policy, Institutions: Papers from the Carnegie-Rochester Conferences on Public Policy*, edited by Karl Brunner and Allan H. Meltzer (Amsterdam: North-Holland; U.S. and Canada: Elsevier Science Publishers, 1983), pp. 165–312.

Nurkse, Ragnar, *Conditions of International Monetary Equilibrium*, Essays in International Finance No. 4 (Princeton, New Jersey: Princeton University Press, 1945).

Obstfeld, Maurice, "Floating Exchange Rates: Performance and Prospects," *Brookings Papers on Economic Activity No. 2* (Washington, 1985), pp. 369–450.

Polak, Jacques J., *Coordination of National Economic Policies*, Occasional Paper No. 7 (New York: Group of Thirty, 1981).

Rogoff, Kenneth, "On the Effects of Sterilized Intervention," *Journal of Monetary Economics* (Amsterdam), Vol. 14 (September 1984), pp. 133–50.

Shafer, Jeffrey R. and Bonnie E. Loopesko, "Floating Exchange Rates After Ten Years," *Brookings Papers on Economic Activity No. 1* (Washington, 1983), pp. 1–70.

Swoboda, Alexander K., "Exchange Rate Regimes and European-U.S. Policy Interdependence," *Staff Papers*, International Monetary Fund (Washington), Vol. 30 (March 1983), pp. 75–102.

Tobin, James, *A Proposal for International Monetary Reform*, Cowles Foundation Discussion Paper No. 506 (New Haven, Connecticut: Yale University Press, 1980).

# REFERENCES

Ungerer, Horst, Owen Evans, and Peter Nyberg, *The European Monetary System: The Experience 1979–82*, Occasional Paper No. 19 (Washington: International Monetary Fund, May 1983).

Willett, Thomas D., *Floating Exchange Rates and International Monetary Reform*, American Enterprise Institute Studies in Economic Policy (Washington: AEI, 1977).

Williamson, John, *The Exchange Rate System* (Washington: Institute for International Economics, 2nd edition, 1985).

Working Group on Exchange Market Intervention, *Report* (unpublished, March 1983).

HG 3881 .C694 1987

CROCKETT, ANDREW.

STRENGTHENING THE
INTERNATIONAL MONETARY

DEC 1 5 1989

DEC 18 1991
JUN 2 '94

MAY 0 2 '95

O'Shaughnessy Library
College of St. Thomas
St. Paul, MN 55105

273633